SOLDIER IN THE CIRCUS

How to Survive Five Years as a Prisoner of War

By
Edward Lyme

Soldier in the Circus

First published1997
The Book Guild Ltd.
25 High Street
Lewes, Sussex
United Kingdom

Email: carolannelyme@aol.co.uk

To
Doris
In memory

'Calais was the crux. *Many other causes might have prevented the deliverance of Dunkirk, but it is certain that the three days gained by the defence of Calais enabled the Gravelines waterline to be held, and that, without this, even in spite of Hitler's vacillations and Rundstedt's orders, all would have been cut off and lost.'*

— Winston S. Churchill, *Their Finest Hour*

Contents

Foreword

M ore than 50 years have elapsed since the end of the Second World War, and one might think that every aspect of that conflict has by now been recorded in official histories, personal accounts and plain fiction.

There has, however, been one facet of the war that has been the subject of so much writing and report from the same source as to present not merely an imbalance but even a totally false picture. Books, films and television series about British prisoners of war in Germany have abounded, and a reader or viewer of a younger generation that has happily not known major war may well believe from these outpourings that British prisoners in German hands divided their time between baiting the guards and digging escape tunnels, for which activity there was always an escape committee for long-term planning.

Virtually all these accounts emanate from officers who in most British regiments represent less than five percent of the personnel. Enlisted men, in British military parlance 'ORs' or Other Ranks, who fell into enemy hands were in a somewhat different situation. They were forced to work, and after a day's work — which may have started well before dawn with a long march to the worksite, then a similar march back after dusk, when they would line up for the one bowl of soup for the day — had neither the time nor much inclination for tunnel digging.

There were escapes, and my own attempts and final success are recorded in the appropriate chapters here, but there was very little in the way of long-term planning, much less tunnel digging, and most escapes from *Stalags* were ad hoc as the opportunity arose. In between, the long-term prisoners spent the early days trying to stay alive and the rest of the time trying to keep sane; in one or two cases known to me, not always with success. In short, the life of Private and junior NCO prisoners was very different from the jolly guard-baiting and escape committees of the Offlags, as depicted in films, and it is for them that I have written this book.

Since this is a personal account, the pages are littered with the well-known upright letter, but this book is not intended to be egotistic. By the end of the battle of France in 1940 the Germans had captured some 30,000 British prisoners, representing about one percent of their total capture of soldiers from Poland, France, Holland, Belgium and some small numbers from Czechoslovakia and Norway. The British total grew to several times the original number by the end of the war. This is their story as well as mine.

E.A.L.

Prologue

The Circus was packed so tightly with humanity it seemed possible to take one's feet from the ground and still remain upright. VE day, 8 May 1945, had brought the crowds from all over London and beyond to celebrate the end of six years of war in Europe, and Piccadilly Circus was the focal point. Everywhere the jubilant throng was solid; the thousands in Piccadilly spread along to Leicester Square to become tens of thousands, then down to Trafalgar Square, through Admiralty Arch, and along the Mall to Buckingham Palace, until there was more than a million people in an unbroken mass from the Circus to the Palace.

Uniforms were everywhere, soldiers, sailors and airmen from a dozen Allied countries and services, and by the nature of the place and occasion British soldiers were predominant.

One of the small scraps of humanity in this mass wore the uniform of a private soldier, a rifleman of the Light Division. He was with his wife, from whom he had been separated for the whole of the war, and was enjoying a private celebration. Five years earlier he had fallen into the hands of the enemy, and had spent the intervening years dreaming of escape or any other circumstance that would bring him back to England before the end of the war. For a Londoner, England meant the capital, and London meant Piccadilly Circus.

Some of the great throng that had converged on the West End that day had started early from the suburbs, others had come from towns in the Home Counties or beyond, and had taken hours to get there. It had taken me five years. But I had made it. This was the day the war in Europe ended, and I was in the Circus.

The *Daily Mirror* cartoon at the time of the battle. The caption reads: "Their Name Liveth for Evermore!"

By permission of the *Daily Mirror*

Edward Lyme, September, 1939. Joining KRRC, aged 21 years.

1

Making up the Numbers

We took a poor view. We, the riflemen of the First Battalion Queen Victoria's Rifles, took a poor view. It was just after midnight on 22 May 1940 and we were about to leave our billets on Wye racecourse to go to war, but that was not the reason for our jaundiced view of the situation. Indeed only five minutes earlier, with the enthusiasm of youth, we were quite excited at the prospect of whatever adventure lay ahead. Admittedly, in retrospect I for one would have been a great deal less keen had I known what did in fact lie ahead, but the future is mercifully hidden from all of us, and when we were roused from our blankets on the floor of the racecourse totalisator to prepare to move to France immediately there was a general air of cheerful bustle. Then the blow fell and the smiles were wiped from all our faces: the bikes would have to be left behind.

At the time the Queen Vics were one of only two battalions in the British Army with motorcycles. One was the regular battalion of the Northumberland Fusiliers, already in France, and the other the Territorial battalion Queen Victoria's Rifles. It is a matter of history that Britain was ill-prepared for a major war, but I wonder if a later generation can understand how bad it really was. In the spring of 1940, six months after war had been declared, the Queen Vics were billeted on Whitbread's Hop Farm at Beltring in Kent, designated as a Motorcycle Battalion but with no motorcycles, and tradesmen's vans to represent non-existent armoured scout cars. At long last in the late spring both scout cars and motorcycle combinations were forthcoming and joy abounded. Apart from the scout cars and despatch riders, the whole battalion was geared to transport by motorcycle combinations, each carrying a driver and two riflemen, except for Bren gunners who travelled individually with a driver. Although it was a light infantry battalion, the drivers were classed as cavalry and had a revolver instead of a rifle. Drivers made up roughly a third of the battalion, and I was one such. I had never actually fired my revolver even in practice, as there was no revolver ammunition; we were told not to draw it except to fire, but as it was empty anyway the instruction seemed superfluous. Eventually in May I was given six rounds of revolver ammunition, just enough to fill the chambers once, and as the battle of France was now under way, I was told to carry it with me always. By this time we had moved from Beltring to Wye, and I remember going to a cinema in Ashford with the revolver sticking out of my trouser pocket, as I had no holster, feeling like a gunslinger from a wild-west film. As I am both clumsy and careless it is a wonder I didn't blow my balls off.

When I joined the Rifles in September 1939 under the original Militia scheme I was already officer trained, having been in my School cadet corps for five years, and as captain of my House shooting team I was a good shot. But like many others in the battalion I was far less interested in soldiering than in driving one of the motorbikes, and I felt providence had indeed smiled on me when the bikes were at last delivered and I was appointed a driver i/c. Furthermore my passenger, Tom Shewring, was a Bren gunner so we had a chummy bike with just two of us. Pretty well all the drivers in the Queen Vics were good drivers and good mechanics; I was neither, and Tom would have been safer with almost anyone else. Still, I kept the thing on the road somehow and was very proud of my status as a driver — I had never driven anything before.

Now, only a few weeks after getting our bikes, we were expected to go to war without them. Life was simply not fair.

Naively, perhaps, we believed that the powers that be knew what they were doing. They didn't, and we were about to be sacrificed in a monumental cock-up on the part of the War Office. The fact that the subsequent loss of a single brigade of rifles at Calais was to bring enormous dividends and prove disproportionately profitable in the scale of war should not be allowed to invest the British Government and its War Office with the presumption of prior knowledge of events or even of their own actions. In the jargon of the day, they hadn't a clue.

The one person who could not be charged with lack of understanding was the new Prime Minister who had only assumed office two weeks earlier, on the very day the German Army launched its offensive against France and the Low Countries. Winston Churchill had spent years in the wilderness unavailingly warning the Government of the German military build-up, but even he had little understanding of the incredible speed of the German advance and the virtual collapse of French resistance. The War Office had no understanding at all and literally at the last minute, as the British and part of the French army were retreating into the Dunkirk perimeter, they decided to make a hasty move to hold the Channel ports of Boulogne and Calais.

Some units of the Guards were sent to Boulogne and their evacuation was ordered on the very day the Rifles were sent to Calais. Such was the measure of the grasp of events displayed on the British side.

No such hesitance attended the German High Command, whose armies had swept through Holland, Belgium and Northern France in less than two weeks, and now — on the day the single battalion of Queen Victoria's Rifles landed at Calais, 22 May 1940 — had already reached the Channel coast and were poised to roll up Boulogne, Calais and Dunkirk. In Dunkirk there were compressed some 330,000 men, comprising the whole British Expeditionary Force of 230,000 and another 100,000 French soldiers.

The following day two more rifle battalions landed, both regular regiments: the 1st Bn Rifle Brigade and 2nd King's Royal Rifle Corps. There was also a tank battalion from the 3rd Royal Tank Regiment. This latter included a young officer named Airey Neave, who was subsequently to achieve fame as an escaper from Colditz and as Member of Parliament — until his tragic death at the hands of IRA terrorists. Airey Neave wrote a full account of the defence of Calais in his book **The Flames of Calais**, published in 1972, and I do not propose to deal with more here than my own part, if part it can be called. The justified praise given by Winston Churchill and others for the stand of the Rifles at Calais, and the many individual deeds of heroism, does not apply to the writer. For all the good I did in holding up the German Army I might as well have stayed at home. Since as a prisoner of war I was not much use to the war effort either, the British nation and Empire might well have been better served if Rifleman Lyme had been left behind. I had only just got married on a five-day leave, and I might at least have produced some progeny who could conceivably have been of some use to the nation in the future.

It was not until many years after the war that I learned the reason why we had to leave our transport behind: the War Office was under the impression that the battalion was 33% larger than it was, and believed there would be no room on the ship for the motorcycles.

We landed at Calais around midday on 21 May 1940 and my company (B Company, Captain Bowring) was ordered to take the farthest post on a perimeter much too large for a battalion of 600 men, of whom only two-thirds had rifles, some six miles along the Sangatte road towards Boulogne, now already in German hands. We arrived there at night and took positions on either side of the road with instructions to let the tanks pass through and fire on the enemy infantry. I lay beside Tom Shewring with his Bren gun as his Number Two in a ditch beside the road, and I remember my feelings well. Only that morning I had been safe in England, and now I must expect to die during the night; I was damn well frightened and only hoped it didn't show. In fact there was nothing to be frightened about; the enemy were still miles away. When they did turn up two days later and I found myself in the middle of a battle, I found it quite exhilarating. Perhaps a psychologist could explain this, but it is not a comforting thought.

The night passed peacefully, and the following morning my platoon was ordered elsewhere. We had no idea where we were going except that it was vaguely further back towards Calais across fields. We eventually arrived at what appeared to be a dilapidated mediaeval castle. This was in fact Fort Nieulay, and was the first bastion in the defence of Calais.

At this time Fort Nieulay was occupied by some 40 French

soldiers under a Captain Herremann, and nearby a makeshift roadblock had been prepared, to be defended by a small detachment of our chaps under Captain Munby QVR. Captain Munby persuaded the French fort commander to let us enter the fort to augment its defence as the roadblock was untenable, so eventually there were about 90 men in the fort, of which about 50 were QVR.

Nothing happened that day, and such was the confusion of our hasty despatch to Calais that after only one full day in France we were already short of rations. This seemed important in the evening, but of no importance at all the following morning when we were attacked by what seemed to me to be half the German Army. This apparent feeling of disproportion was not perhaps all that far wrong. Fort Nieulay was in the path of the German 1st Armoured Division and 86th Rifle Regiment, with supporting artillery assisted by Stukas of the Luftwaffe. `The defence of Fort Nieulay between the Germans and Calais was of critical importance in the next few hours.' (Airey Neave, **The Flames of Calais**).

It started with rifle and machine-gun fire, which for the most part zipped harmlessly over our heads and gave me a detached and semi-thrilling interest in finding myself in the sounds of war without apparently being in any real danger. I was brought suddenly and horribly to reality when my left-hand neighbour, Corporal Chennelles — with whom, against regulations, I had shared a blanket for warmth on our last night in England — incautiously raised his head and had his face virtually sliced in two by a machine-gun burst.

Thereafter the pounding never ceased, and the artillery bombardment became so severe that Captain Munby ordered all except one Bren gun into one of the fort's cellars. As Tom had the No.1 Bren, this meant that he and I, with the Platoon commander

Lieutenant Nelson and the platoon sergeant, Sgt Osborne, went to the topmost mound of the fort while everyone else went below. As I write this many years later I half wonder if I am imagining my own feelings at the time, but I know I am not. I remember very well. As the four of us took position on the top of the fort, I wished I was one of the others going down to the cellars and hoped we would not be there long. But once in position a strange exhilaration took over, and although personal feelings were not mentioned I am sure it was the same for the other three.

We were supposed to wait until enemy infantry got close enough to be a good target for this solitary Bren. But the French, who were still manning the lower walls, opened fire with a heavy machinegun when the Germans were still out of sight so far as I was concerned (in fact I never saw them clearly until they were a yard to two away and I put my hands up) and I heard my platoon commander curse them for bloody fools. Certainly the Germans went to ground but continued to fire on us, and both French and British sustained casualties during this period, although our little quartet on the top seemed to have a charmed life.

At one point Lt Nelson handed me his binoculars to see if I could locate a machine-gun which was plaguing us and which so far we had not found. Like an idiot, instead of raising my head cautiously I popped my head up high and immediately a line of machine-gun rounds stitched the parapet a few inches below my head.

Following this Sgt Osborne ('Ernie') decided he would like to take a hand with the Bren. He took over from Tom Shewring and surprised me by ignoring the rules he had spent months drilling into the rest of us. 'Always short bursts' was the drill. Ernie took no notice of this. He fired six magazines straight off with his finger tight on the trigger and as a result the barrel got red hot.

Now this is where drill comes in. I was acting as his No.2, and according to the drill the No.2 on the words `Change Barrels' whips off the barrel, puts on a new one, clips it tight and the gun is ready for firing again. In practice one was allowed ten seconds for this, but it was quite easy to do it in six — according to the book, that is.

`Change Barrels!' called Ernie. Easy. I had spare barrels beside me and with the professionalism of long practice flipped up the catch and slid the barrel forward. But it didn't slide forward. The bloody thing wouldn't come off. It was too hot. I tugged and swore but to no avail. It wouldn't budge.

I wish someone could have photographed the scene that followed. We got the thing down into a hollow and Ernie and I sat on the ground holding opposite ends of the Bren with our feet together tugging at the thing and laughing like a couple of schoolboys. Although the shelling and mortaring continued we were not worried by that particular machine-gun again, so Ernie may well have got it with his six magazines.

Our little topmost group of four had been very lucky so far, but there is a limit to how far you can push your luck, and as the shelling showed no sign of abating Lt Nelson decided we should loin the others in the cellar, which was just as well. The bombardment increased to an incredible intensity. Although I did not know it, this was the final German attack, and when they were almost at the gate the French Commander decided further resistance was useless and surrendered.

The Germans streamed into the fort and surrounded the entrance to the cellar, ordering us out. I happened to be nearest the door, and took my revolver out of my holster (for the first time!). With my finger on the trigger but with my hands in the air I came out into daylight. It was ridiculous, and I have no idea, nor had I any idea then, what I intended to do — to shoot someone, to shoot myself, or just to act plain stupid. If I intended anything dramatic, it failed.

A young German holding a Schmeisser indicated that a pistol was not desirable and I meekly pulled my lanyard over my head and handed it to him. So far as I know this action gave me the doubtful honour — or ignominy — of being the first rifleman to be captured at Calais.

It will be clear that the defence of Fort Nieulay was affected by the other 89 men — Rfn Lyme being there solely for the purpose of making up the numbers. Their efforts, and the sacrifice of casualties, British and French, should not go unrecorded. Fort Nieulay held up two German divisions, one of them armoured, for 11 hours.

Calais town held out for another two days, during which time the Gravelines Waterlines were flooded, securing the flank of the British and French troops at Dunkirk, from where a third of a million men were taken by the small boats to England. So in the scale of war the sacrifice of the Rifles at Calais was worthwhile. I could still have done without it.

* * *

As we emerged from Fort Nieulay the scene was much changed from the bare countryside I had viewed from the top of the fort. The whole area was swarming with tanks, all descending from the hill before the fort and past it towards Calais, with infantry and lorries streaming down the Calais road. We were told to start walking up this road, and a kind gentleman with a potato-masher raised above his head indicated that he would throw it amongst us if we didn't move. We moved.

How far we moved I have no idea. We started as a small group, but were either joined by or joined more and ever more French prisoners on what seemed an endless march. The column did not seem to grow behind us, only lengthening more and more in front, until the whole road ahead as far as one could see was a moving mass of French with the small contingent of British ever at the rear. We simply kept putting one foot in front of the other until at what appeared to be around midnight we were herded into a field covered with prone bodies sleeping the sleep of exhausted men. I could not see anywhere to lie down — there was no grass, only men — until at last I spied a gap between two French soldiers. As I reached it I saw why it was a gap — it was full of cow pats. I couldn't care less, and flopped down and went to sleep. When I was roused the next morning, some of this ambrosia had adhered to my battledress, but I do not recall finding anything offensive about it. When I later found one or two of my own kind from the platoon no one else remarked on it either, so either we all smelt the same or, more probably, we were too full of our own misery to worry about anyone else.

For the next three weeks we marched on and on and ever on. From the pervading weariness and constant hunger of that period odd incidents spring to mind.

The second day was the day I surprised myself with my expertise as a pickpocket. We had all flopped down by the roadside in one of the half-hour breaks. The normal marching procedure of the British Army is (or was then) a ten-minute break in an hour's march. The Germans appeared to keep the same basic intention but with two-and-a-half hours' marching with a half-hour break to follow. This meant that by the time one got the break one was pretty well exhausted, especially as we enjoyed this amusement from dawn until well after dusk. On this occasion I tried the experiment of getting up after a very short rest, little as I felt like moving, as it seemed to me it was harder to get up if you flopped out completely for the half-hour.

I moved around a little and noticed a German guard sitting on a low bank beside the road with his back towards me and with what was clearly a tin of bully-beef protruding from his trouser pocket. I strolled over and sat beside him for a few minutes, then got up and moved away. The tin was now in my pocket.

When we started off again I was delighted to find myself marching beside Ernie Osborne, and proudly told him of my acquisition. He said he too could contribute, and reaching down into the front pocket of his battledress produced a large crust of stale bread. It looked as though it had been buried in the earth and then rubbed on the roadway to ensure the maximum adherence of dirt, but it was a joyful sight and would be the right complement to my own ill-gotten gain.

Before we were to enjoy this feast, however, I was to experience a new depth of unforeseen misery.

It was only just after this pick-pocketing break that the sky clouded over and it was clear that it would rain. Many of the French seemed well equipped for the march, but almost without exception the British — my own platoon of the QVR and others we gradually met along the way who had been taken prisoner elsewhere — were captured with the battledress they stood up in and nothing else.

When the rain started it proved to be a real humdinger of a storm. Not one of your brief storms followed by the sunshine and the birds twittering. This one went on and on, already dark in the afternoon, with dramatic flashes of lightning in the soaked fields either side, for hour after hour. And we too went on and on. No break, just on along an endless road. I can remember to this day, 55 years later, the worst part that seemed to me like a water torture. My battledress was soaked, I was soaked, I was dead tired, but worst of all was the drip drip inside my battledress blouse into the small of my back.

Notwithstanding the rain, we were all thirsty. By this time the huge column, one of many in France, included French, Belgians, Dutch and — still in a minority — British, and when we passed through a village all could be seen jostling with one another to get their mouths under the streams of water from gutter overflows.

At long last we staggered into a town and into what was clearly the marketplace with an equestrian statue in the centre. Here the column was breaking up, with groups of men lying all round the square. There seemed no place for me anywhere, with or without cowpats, and I somehow made my way to the top step round the statue. It was narrow but at least clear. This was in fact the town of Montreuil, headquarters of the British Expeditionary Force of the First World War, and the statue was that of the British Commander-in-Chief, Field Marshal Haig.

By the time I found my little haven of rest it had stopped raining, and although it involved a little careful balancing I managed to compose my carcass along the top step for sleep. I was dead tired and thought that nothing could stop me sleeping; I am sure more rain or thunder or gunfire would not have stopped me. But there was something else. The recumbent forms around the base of the statue were all Belgian soldiers, some of them chatting to each other in some language which was certainly not French so I presumed must be Flemish. Somehow this drone in an incomprehensible language was too much. I was not going to be able to sleep here. I stood up. I was too high on the plinth to step down gently. I would have to jump, and the whole base of the statue and the surrounding square was a solid carpet of human bodies. I simply couldn't jump on one of them. Yes I could; and I jumped and ran. I am sure the words that followed me would have been an interesting addition to the vocabulary in any language, but I was away from that damn statue. I found a gap in the bodies somewhere and slept.

The following day I found Ernie and we shared the bully-beef and bread. Nor was that to be all. Although we were to march for some three weeks from dawn to dusk every day, that morning in Montreuil after the rain was to be the start of a two-day break from marching in which a half-dozen of us were to dine and sleep at the equivalent of The Ritz.

Around mid-day all the prisoners were roused up to start marching again, but to our surprise we only marched just outside the town and into a large field. There must have been many thousands of prisoners in this field, and Ernie and I found another four members of the platoon of QVR here. We had not been there long when a German NCO came into the field and over to our little group of half-a-dozen. He had not especially chosen us, we just happened to be near the gate. We were told to follow him.

We were led back into Montreuil square, now empty of prisoners but littered with rubbish. He led us to one of the buildings in the square and up the stairs inside. It was only a small shop with a flat above it, but the upper rooms were full of wooden cases, some of them marked *Pain-de-Guerre*, the French army hard-tack. He indicated that we were to carry these cases down the narrow stairs and put them on a lorry outside — we were to be careful not to damage them.

Since the cases were wooden and we had no tools it took a little ingenuity to damage them, but we managed it and found that some contained interesting tins. The cases of hard-tack were a little stronger and we had to accidentally drop one of these cases down the stairs to break it open. Our German guard was clearly a soldier's soldier and looked the other way as we loaded the cases. The result of this assistance to the Wehrmacht was that when the job was finished we had all put on weight. Our battle-dress blouses were stuffed with hard-tack and tins of salmon and bully-beef.

Nor was that all for our comfort that day. As we were about to be led back to the field outside the town, we looked around the littered square and found a huge and heavy carpet, about 12 feet square. We stood in line and rolled this up and between us we carried it back to the field. We then sat down to a meal of hard-tack and tinned salmon, probably the only prisoners to dine that day.

In addition to the Great Carpet we had found some canvas which we had brought back, and after our Ritzy meal we laid the canvas down as a ground sheet and pulled the carpet over us — it was large enough to cover all six of us together. I went to sleep and woke during the night to find it was pouring with rain again with thousands of men standing round in rain and misery. I do not recall that I felt any pity for my fellow men. I was thankful I was All Right Jack, and drew my head under the carpet again, like a tortoise into its shell.

The following morning it was on with the march again. We were able to treat ourselves to some bully-beef breakfast, first, and I kept a square of the canvas which I hung on to until I got a greatcoat issued months later. I was determined not to suffer my wet misery again. The carpet, which must have weighed a hundredweight, had to be left behind in the field. But it had served a noble purpose.

Then came the long march every day and, once the perks of

Montreuil had gone, the constant hunger and thirst and weariness, all now happily long ago and mostly forgotten. But some things are still vivid in memory.

There was the constant passage west of the Germany army. The sight for the first time of huge half-track personnel carriers; why hadn't we got any of these? The open-backed trucks with steaming cauldrons aboard and cooks preparing stew for the troops at the end of the journey; why hadn't we thought of this? The long lines of tanks, with the occasional tankman leaning over his turret and tapping the side, calling out derisively in English, 'Cardboard tanks, eh Tommy?' The vehicle drivers with cigars sticking out of their mouths (smoking was not allowed in the British army when driving). The soldiers on the half-tracks cheerfully pointing out to each other the small British group at the end of the long French columns, calling, 'Tommies, Tommies!' and snapping us with their cameras (cameras were also forbidden in the British army). But most of all, I recall the impression of sheer numbers and the power of a conquering army. And Churchill had expected me to stop this lot with a revolver! Like all the rest of the British I ever met on the march or in the prison camp, it never occurred to me at any time we would not eventually win the war, but it was going to be a long haul.

The British always seemed to be at the end of these columns, and once I found myself literally at the end. There were two of us — one's companion was the chap nearest at any time, and constantly changing as we plodded on — with just one other behind us and behind him the follow-up truck, which to add insult to injury was a captured 30 cwt British Army Bedford with a machine gun mounted on it. The three of us were limping from blisters and the guard on the truck called out to us to get a move on. We still limped. Suddenly there was a brief burst of machine-gun fire and we glanced back to see that the rearmost man had been shot dead and a marching guard had kicked his body aside for the truck to pass. We suddenly found a burst of speed and were quickly in the middle of the British contingent. I never got to the very back again.

By this time a pattern had been established by French house-wives in the villages we passed through, which continued all the time we were in France. It was a blazing hot summer and we were constantly thirsty. As the columns passed through the villages there was always a group of Frenchwomen standing outside their houses with pails, bowls and saucepans of water. The column never stopped, but the French and other captives were able to scoop up water in their cans as they passed. As soon as the British came in sight the German guards called out `*Englander nichts*' and either knocked us away with rifle butts or kicked the pails over. Any soldier who was on that march will remember this, as it was a constant source of discussion and lack of understanding. Did they hate us that much? Was it just bloody-mindedness? Or was it, as some more charitable chaps thought, because French water was not supposed to be good for British stomachs?

There was another problem for us in the simple lack of a receptacle for food or water, since as already mentioned most of us were taken with only what we stood up in. As the march proceeded the British could be seen with a most odd assortment of drinking vessels hanging from their tunics — tin cans, jugs, cracked china cups, and even one or two genuine mess tins. One chap had a large chamber pot.

In one town square where we halted and flopped out tempo-rarily I saw a young girl going round the prisoners near me selling cuts of cheese. Whether this was a genuine commercial venture or simply an act of kindness with the insistence of sale only a token, I cannot say. The only coin I had was an English sixpence, and she was quite prepared to take this, for which I received a small and very ripe Camembert. After the brief windfall 'won' at Montreuil, this was the only instance — other than the incident of the caraway seed later — when I can remember getting some private food.

It was in this same square that the whole noise of the packed mass of prisoners, still mostly French, died down to listen to a tiny group of Irish guardsmen in one corner singing 'Danny Boy'. The moment passed, but you didn't have to be Irish to be left with a heartfelt reminder of home.

On another occasion, after being herded into a field in the evening, a long line suddenly formed behind a large tin bath with steam coming from it. There was no point in going to look at the bath, the important thing was to get in the queue quickly, which I did. The word was that the Germans had provided a barley stew. When I got up to the bath it only contained once-hot and now tepid water. It was quite clear water, and whether it ever contained any barley was debatable, but on the basis that it had once contained something that might perhaps have exuded some form of nutriment into the water I took my share and hoped it might do me some good.

Yet another field some days and much marching later was the scene of the caraway seed incident. I was mooching round the field with another QVR — names on the march fade with the years — when we saw trodden into the earth a tiny biscuit. We levered it out and it proved to be a French army hard-tack biscuit. These biscuits were quite different from ours, being small and thick, almost like a lozenge, and of course very hard. It was near impossible to halve such an object, but by careful biting we managed to do this, to have half each. There was, however, a measure of disproportion. We had managed to bite this normally unappetising object into almost exact halves, but one half had protruding from it the end of a caraway seed. We took this out, ate our respective halves, and then discussed the seed. Did it contain anything that might do our bodies any good? Probably not, we decided, but fair is still fair. Using the same technique with the edge of the teeth as in the case of the original biscuit we managed to halve it, making it probably the only caraway seed in history to be shared between two persons.

Then of course, the next day, on with the march. The March. In my Stalag of 20,000 prisoners, all taken in France in 1940, any conversation during the next five years which contained any reference to those early days was simplified by those two words. We were drawn from different parts of the United Kingdom, often antagonistic to other regions or regiments, with different personal stories of battle or circumstances of capture, but The March was common to all. The experience was so strongly stamped in the mind of every participant that five years later when we marched west in similar long columns under very much worse climatic conditions on a much longer route for a much longer period and with many more deaths, the natural discussions of comparison still referred to the long trail winding into captivity as The March.

In the happier days of the QVR at Beltring Hop Farm a century earlier — could it really have been only last month? — I had been particularly chummy with one Dennis Hoy, and had pleasant memories of his parents visiting on Sunday and taking us both to tea. He was in a different Company and therefore captured two days later than I was in Calais town, but we met up again on the march, and stayed together for the rest of the march and the first year of captivity. It was with Denis that my own march finally came to an end.

We were in the inevitable field one evening, both hobbling as we had considerable blisters, when the guards went round the field looking for anyone 'sick'. There were of course some who were quite ill, but most of those so classed were limpers, pretty well all from the same cause. We were led in a hobbling bunch out of the field and down the road, presumably to a dressing station for treatment. There was no such dressing station, no treatment, but something much more welcome. There was a train. It was not exactly Pullman comfort. We were motioned to get onto an open flat unsided wagon, and once on it found it almost impossible to sit or lie down, as it was laced with large beams like sleepers at short intervals at right angles to the wagon base. Never mind, the weight was off our feet, and we managed to drape ourselves in some manner round or along these obstacles and rest.

The train made a start but at some time in the night was halted for an hour or so. There were a number of German soldiers standing around at the point of halt, and one wretched *Gefreiter* (Lance Corporal) chose to show off his languages. There was only our wagon with British aboard, the rest of the train had French prisoners, and this cocky character chose to come up to our wagon and ask in English what we were doing on the train. I think it was Denis who told him we were sick, and he then addressed the French prisoners on the wagons next to us to tell them what rotten soldiers the British were, leaving all the fighting to the French and pretending to be sick. All in all he did not regard us with favour. As far as I could see, the French took no notice of him — either his French was not as good as he thought or, more likely, they, like ourselves, were too wrapped up in their own worries to care one way or another. Seeing he was not making the impression a conqueror ought to make, he turned quite nasty and, waving a pistol about, ordered us off the wagon for work. Most of the occupants of this wagon could hardly walk, but he made us move a few yards down the train and move a few sleepers from one pile to another. We did not do much of this as the train was about to start again, and since he really had nothing to do with us he had to let us climb back on to the wagon, shouting at us that once we got to Germany we would be made to work until we dropped and so would all the British once the war was won, which would be soon. Little mean-minded men with little authority and a loud mouth are the same everywhere, and we were too tired to take much notice of him, but it was still less than cheering to roll off to Germany with that in our ears. I dozed off miserably.

The world looked quite different when I awoke. The sun was shining and the train was rolling through countryside that was taken straight from a child's picture book. Green well-tended fields, neat little red-roofed cottages, all a totally different aspect from the dusty roads of the past three weeks. We soon knew where we were when the train steamed into a main station and stopped. The legend on the station nameboard was Luxembourg. It was to be many years before I was to visit Luxembourg, both on holiday and business, and to find it as pleasant a town as it looked that morning in the sunshine from the deck of an open wagon.

We were the object of the usual interest in 'Tommies' from a troop train standing on the opposite platform, but we did not stay long in Luxembourg station. The train moved on and later the same day stopped at another large station where we were all motioned to get off. This was Trier, and although I would not have known the word then, it was the first town in Germany with a *Dulag*. The word is short for *Durchlager*, which means literally a passing through camp, a place for sorting out nationalities for onward transmission to appropriate more permanent camps

— *Offlags* for officers, *Malags* for seamen, *Luftlags* for airmen and of course *Stalags* (short for *Stammlager*) for enlisted soldiers. We moved in a long column through the town to the base of the long and steep hill, where there was a German soldier beside a Red Cross vehicle calling out to ask if there was anyone sick who needed transport to the camp on top of the hill. I cannot analyse my feelings in this long retrospect — maybe we were just being pigheaded, but both Denis and I ignored this offer and walked up that bloody hill, which seemed at the time to go on forever.

Eventually we arrived at the top and entered the *Dulag*. We had only just got inside the gate when we saw one of our own regiment, who called out to us that this was a marvellous place, they gave you bread and jam. I do not remember whether we ever got the bread and jam because we were only there one night, and then went down that hill again to another train.

This time the train was all covered box-cars; this time the prisoners were all British; and this time the guards were all swines. We were hurried into the box-cars with rifle butts, the doors were slammed and bolted and we started a journey that in a different way was worse than the march. I think we were given one loaf between five men once during a three-day journey — now moving, now shunted on a side line, but always moving eastwards. We realised our destination was Poland long before we got there; it had to be, no train could keep on forever travelling east.

At last we stopped at a station signboarded Thorn. This was the German name for the old Polish town of Torun, the birthplace of Copernicus, and a town ringed with forts built in the nineteenth century as a then-modern bastion against the east. We were herded into lines and through the gates of a grim-looking fortress near the railway line. This was Fort 17.

We had arrived at Stalag XXA.

2

Kilts and Bread Pudding

Food, blessed food. As we entered Fort 17 we were lined up in rows of five. In those early days, when there were large numbers of prisoners to count, this system of fives had a double convenience; it was easier to count and simple to hand a load of bread to the leading file for `Funf Mann ein Brot'. The German loaf of black rye bread was a fairly solid object which we later found was exactly five times as long as the width of the metal identity disc issued to us, and after the issue of these identifications the loaf was always shared by cutting to the width of the disc.

Since it was well known by this time that the Rifles had been captured after a single battle at Calais, it became a standard joke in the Stalag to say that the Rifles had marched off the boat in fives. This took such root that it was trotted out every now and then during the whole five years of captivity in Stalag XXA, and a friend has even reminded me of it in later years. The jest was made and received in perfectly good humour, although if they heard it in the shades those who died at Calais may have felt it to be a little unfair.

The prisoners' accommodation in Fort 17 was a little different from the other forts. In Fort 13 (the headquarters fort for the Stalag), Fort 14 (the hospital fort) and Fort 16 (prison fort, commonly known as 'the Bunker'), the prisoners slept in the fort itself; I was in all of them at some time or another, and the most optimistic estate agent could not have described them as desirable residences. In Fort 17 the prisoners slept in huts in the grounds and had to climb a steep slope to the latrine trenches on the top of the fort. The wooden bunks were not the luxurious one-up and one-down type depicted in so many films and television portrayals of prison camp life. Indeed I did not sleep in such a bunk until I had been a prisoner more than a year. The bunks in Fort 17 and in others I slept in during my early captivity were built to accommodate large numbers at one time and consisted of long wooden shelves, usually three tiers high, where the prisoners could lie down in long rows side by side.

Denis and I found a corner on one of the upper shelves, and this was to be our home for the next few weeks. I believe we were issued with a blanket apiece and that was about our lot. Not that it mattered. There was only one thing that mattered, and that was food. The pattern that was quickly established and was to last for the next five years was one bowl of soup a day with a ration of bread, always five men to a loaf. There was a brief period when the black loaves issued were thickly green with mould, having been in store apparently from several wars back. Oddly enough this green mouldy bread was well received, as in order to get rid of it the Germans gave us a loaf between three men while it lasted, so we felt a little better off with it than the normal ration.

In this camp the soup was issued at around eleven o'clock in the morning, although it took a couple of hours for the whole camp to go through. We were issued with spoons but had to find our own receptacles. The soup was potato or swede, and twice a week was 'meat' day. I did get a piece of horse's meat in my soup once or twice, but I do not think my mother would have approved of the quality.

The prisoners in this camp not only encompassed a wide range of the regiments of the British army, but also some RAF ground staff who had been caught up, and a lot of Poles, who were already there when we arrived. This was the only camp where this mixture applied, and in due course the RAF and the Poles went elsewhere.

There was a fairly large contingent of Scotsmen, almost all from the Argyle and Sutherland Highlanders, who were caught at St. Valery when the famous 51st Division was surrounded there. Most British regiments have a song of their own, and it was here that I heard the song 'It's an Argyle for me'. These Army songs are frequently no more than permutations of the songs sung by other regiments, and I got so used to the Argyle's song it was a genuine surprise to me later to hear the Gordons singing exactly the same song altered to 'It's a Gordon for me'. (My own original regiment, the King's Royal Rifle Corps, also had its own song which could hardly be said to be one of blowing our own trumpet. It included the line: 'We cannot fight, we cannot shoot, what bloody use are we?')

The Scotsman's kilt was of course an object of some specula-tion among the Poles. One day after the soup had been issued I saw a little group of Poles discussing a Scotsman they saw sitting on a bank with his legs splayed out and his bowl in his lap eating his soup. Finally one of the Poles left the group and strolled past. As he drew level he dropped something and in bending down to pick it up, looked up the Scotman's kilt. He then returned to his colleagues and reported. If you want to know what he reported you will have to drop something yourself, or ask a Scotsman.

(I experienced a strange parallel to this incident several years later when I was on holiday with my wife and family in Spain. This was in the early days of Spanish tourism when the seaside town we stayed at — Lloret-de-Mar — was still a village, and when it was forbidden to leave the beach in a bathing costume or swimming trunks even to cross the road. We had taken a trip inland, and I was wearing a pair of white cotton shorts. We stopped at a small village and I soon found a small crowd following me, amused and perhaps shocked, to see an Englishman walking about in broad daylight evidently in his underwear. We stopped at the cafe and sat down for a drink, and while I was there a villager would walk past every now and then, drop a coin, and look under the table to see my 'underwear'.)

There were some unfortunate side effects from the change of diet, one of which concerned the bowels. There were around 2000 men in this camp, and a good half of this number found they had to get up in the night, in some cases several times, and climb the ramp up to the latrines. After the long march, the train journey, and now short commons, we were very weak and many made this journey on all fours. I was fortunate in not being affected in this way, but I was among the minority. Maybe my plumbing system coped better, or maybe I just have a large bowel. Certainly I was thankful I didn't have to toil up that slope each night.

Other effects were more serious. Sometimes a man walking about normally in the morning would find that his knee would swell up like a balloon in the afternoon, and he would be quite unable to walk for a week or two. Although this did not happen to me in this camp, I did have a bout of it in the next camp. Fortunately this did not seem to have any lasting effect and the knee eventually went back to normal.

The ulcers were much worse, and affected a large number of men. They appeared most often on the legs and arms — particularly the legs — and many chaps were in a shocking and painful state for weeks and even months with them. Like most other ailments, such excrescences healed with the passage of time, but there will be many ex-prisoners who bear the scars to this day. In this matter, too, I was lucky and the plague passed me by.

In such a state the one daily meal was obviously of the greatest importance, and one would think it impossible that anyone should voluntarily forgo his bowl of soup. But if one could get hold of a cigarette there was always someone willing to pass over his soup ticket for it. Like most soldiers I smoked before capture, but I not only found it easy to give it up when there was nothing to smoke, I was not even interested while my belly was empty. This was not the case with many others — and these, remember, were not old men hardened to a lifetime's smoking, but all young men. It was quite a lesson in the hold that cigarettes can take on a man. I think in my own case it was made easier by the fact that although I had smoked both cigarettes and a pipe as a young man, I was really a pipesmoker and did not inhale. The lack of cigarettes therefore did not hit me as hard as it did others.

Cigarettes were not all that was missing; my hair went missing also. Our heads were shaven, and although this may be an admirable practice for cleanliness, we did not take kindly to it. In my case I got hold of a cigarette from somewhere and passed this valuable item to the barber, who obliged me by leaving a tiny circle of hair about two inches in diameter at the front of my forehead. I religiously parted this each morning with my hands and felt a great deal more civilised and normal with a little hair on my head.

On the other hand hardly anyone had shaved during the long

march for lack of razors, and I had a beard. Not, I am afraid, one of your luxurious beards giving that manly, piratical look usually associated with the Royal Navy; more of a pathetic straggling bumfluff. One chap had managed to bring with him a Rolls Razor and he shaved a large number of the camp with this, including me. I do not remember under what circumstances I acquired a razor, but I eventually got one and never grew a beard again.

It was in this first camp, with my shaven head — with its little parting of two inches in front, of course — and my unshaven face, that I was photographed, complete with a frame dangling from my neck bearing my *Kriegsgefangene* number 8075. These photos were then mounted on a card with personal particulars on the front and a space on the back for recording any criminal convictions that might arise during captivity. I would very much like to have had that card, not only for the memento of a photograph that would not look out of place in the archives of Dartmoor prison, but also for the fact that in due course I collected a record on the back after a conviction for escaping. But all that lay ahead, in those early days in Fort 17.

Although Fort 17 was a part of Stalag XXA, it could be seen later that for most of us it was merely a transit camp where prisoners could be registered and sorted out for *Arbeitskommandos* (working parties). During the two months I was at Fort 17 we were occasionally put into parties to go out and do some work, but it was clearly for the sake of finding us something to do. The first time I went out in this way I went to a stone quarry bashing stones into smaller stones. I really felt like a convict on that one. On another occasion a small party of us were taken to a kitchen garden and given hoes with instructions to hoe out all the weeds growing between rows of cabbages. The guard was less than amused to find that I had hoed out the cabbages and left the weeds. This was not from bloodymindedness on my part, rather a complete uselessness at anything agricultural. I was not sent to the kitchen garden again.

It was at Fort 17 that we were able to send our first letter-card home; we were allowed one lettercard and two postcards a month. Since there was of course strict censorship it became difficult as time passed to find something useful to say; there is a limit to the permutations of `I am still all right'. The first letter, however, presented no difficulties at all. We were told we could later receive parcels from home, and did not know at that time how limited these parcels would be or that food would not be allowed, so everyone wrote home for food. Of course we talked about food a great deal, and someone once remarked how much he missed his mother's thick, greasy bread pudding. Somehow this caught on, and we all had visions of tucking into a large baking tin full of bread pudding! The essence of this vision was that the article should be thick and greasy. I did not specify this, but as I didn't get it, the wish remained academic anyway.

By September 1940, we had been at this fort for about two months when Denis and I found ourselves ordered with others to prepare to move to an *Arbeitskommando*. Few people could have moved with all their belongings from one address to another with as little preparation. Our worldly possessions consisted of a blanket, a mess-tin or whatever equivalent we had managed to equip ourselves with, a spoon, and in my case, my invaluable filthy square of canvas carried all the way from Montreuil. This item was dear to me and jealously guarded, as it served both as ground sheet and my only protection from the elements until such time, if ever, we might be issued with greatcoats.

These *Arbeitskommandos* came to be called 'Transports' by the British, and there were 280 of us on this one. We entrained at Thorn in the usual cattle trucks in the morning, and arrived at dusk at a tiny station called Rittel. We marched some distance and stopped at what later proved to be about a kilometre from the village of Rittel with only open fields around, surrounded in their turn by the thick fir forests to be found throughout Poland. This was it, we were told. What was it? This. The field. This was our camp.

We were herded into the field for the night, and I can remember even now how grateful I was for my canvas, which Denis and I were able to use as a ground sheet with the blankets above.

For some time we slept in this field each night as we gradually built the camp. I found it particularly galling, and indeed almost the depths of ignominy, to build a barbed-wire fence. Even the beasts of the field cannot be forced to build their own cage. Then followed the huts — one for the Kommandant, one for the guards, and four for the prisoners — plus a cookhouse.

The huts had two rooms, one a communal room and one a sleeping room. This latter only had one 'bed', a wooden two-tier structure where 70 men were to sleep in rows as at the *Stalag* — the only choice being this side or that, bottom or top. Denis and I staked a claim to a top position, which was only a matter of a foot or so under the sloping roof. Top bunks, with no one sleeping above, always seemed to be a little freer than the bottom positions, which were generally regarded as more favourable. These things matter in a prison camp.

It seemed we were to work on building a new road, the very road beside which the camp was established. I never knew or cared where the road came from or where it went; it existed, the work existed, my captivity existed, and I was damn well determined to continue to exist myself — until this nightmare was over and I would be free again. I am not sure whether if I had known then how long it would be I would have made it.

The working hours would not have appealed to a shop steward of the Transport and General Workers' Union. We were roused well before dawn, paraded and counted, marched some miles to the work site, worked, marched back, and arrived at around dusk for our one meal of the day, usually barley or swede soup. Continuing the *Stalag* pattern, the soup might or might not contain meat in accordance with the day of the week; some were designated 'meat days' and others 'meatless days'.

Although the village was only a kilometre away, we always marched in the opposite direction, and for the first few months I only saw Rittel at a distance. It was a small and fairly poor village, but it had a church with an onion dome, the first I had seen. The first time I saw it, it looked so oriental, so different from any church I was used to, that it made me feel very far from home.

I was a rotten worker. If the Third Reich had depended on workers like me they would have lost the war earlier than they did. The work we did on the road requires no description other than to say that no matter what the task for the day was, it involved shovelling something from A to B. There were two types of shovel: one short-handled, which was easier to work with, and one long-handled, which was more laborious to work with but more suited to leaning on. I was a long-shovel man. Of course I got chased for that every now and again by the guards, and most chaps reckoned it was easier to work than to lounge. They had a point; dodging the column can be hard work. The British never got this work-dodging down to the fine art of the Poles. I remember one particular long mound of sand which seemed self-perpetuating, as there was always a long line of Poles shovelling it but it never seemed to get smaller. They had the art, which I found by experiment requires constant application, of very slowly digging the shovel in the sand, very slowly lifting the shovel with a small amount of sand on it, slowly placing it on the new heap, and slowly returning to repeat the operation. Done by a long line of shovellers, all working at a dead-slow rate, this gives an impression of a hive of industry with shovel blades flashing to and fro in an apparent orgy of work. I admired the Poles.

Summer passed into autumn and into the early winter of November, the time of the Lazy Wind. By this time we had been issued with greatcoats, all of them from stock captured by the Germans in France or the Low Countries, and we really looked a rag-bag mixture with blue coats of the Dutch army and the different browns and khakis of Belgian and French coats. Most of these had already seen better days, but I got a new Belgian greatcoat. I was not as grateful as no doubt I should have been, as the style involved a flared skirt and it seemed too feminine to me. Still it was a coat, but not enough to keep one sheltered from The Wind.

Polish winters can be very cold indeed, with temperatures only readable on the thermometer by standing on the head, but that first November was a particularly wretched cold time. The icy wind, emanating from the Steppes of Russia hundreds of miles to the east, numbed the whole body. Somebody christened this the Lazy Wind because it was too lazy to go round you and went straight through you, and the name stuck. Several times the guard had to take his rifle off his shoulder to stop men standing about shivering and make them get some work done. There were even a couple of occasions when the guard fired a shot over our heads, but this was very rare; when you are a weaponless prisoner and the enemy has a rifle, he need do no more than take it off his shoulder to be understood.

The cold wind had a least one beneficial effect; it kept the lice at bay. By this time we were thoroughly alive with lice in the warmth of the hut back in the camp, but out in the wind the little buggers kept quiet. When we got back to the camp, and after drawing soup (which was always the first consideration), de-lousing was the order of the day. There were different methods for this, according to personal taste. Most of us simply took our shirts and trousers off, pulled them inside-out, and went louse-hunting among the seams with our hands, cracking our captures between thumb nails. Others preferred to convey them carefully to the top of the hot stove and watch them run about for a moment or two before popping. Another method was to take the oil lamp and run it along the seams, but this burnt the material. I swear I once watched a man hold the lamp underneath his private parts for his personal de-lousing; he must have been very tough indeed, but probably even in that early stage already a bit 'wire-happy'. One way or another we hunted the lice down, and when a man found two together he would call out so that we could congratulate two lice on dying at such a beautiful moment.

We were eventually taken to a local town to be de-loused in the hospital. We had looked forward to this as a break from the camp and as a means of getting rid of our visitors, but it proved on the whole to be a miserable occasion. For most of the day we hung about shivering in a small courtyard, going into the hospital in small batches to shower and wait while our one and only battledress went through the de-louser, which put the clothes through intense heat and sulphur fumes. When we got them back, scorched and stinking of sulphur, we had to go back to the cold courtyard so that others could have their turn.

During this wait in the courtyard on de-lousing day I asked permission to go into the hospital to the toilet. This was granted, and when I entered it — a normal common-or-garden lavatory with tiled walls and urinal stalls — the placed looked so clean that I felt out of place in my filthy battledress, which had not been off my back for months. I felt that if anyone came in during the few moments I was there they would immediately have me thrown out, as this beautiful place was clearly meant for humans to use and not the likes of me. I had indeed sunk low.

And it was all a waste of time. When we got back to the camp we happily shook dead lice from our now de-loused uniforms, but presumably lice eggs are made of sterner stuff, and we were quite soon alive again. Some chaps tried killing them by the opposite form of treatment, leaving their shirts out on the barbed wire overnight when the temperature was well below zero. But like the heat and sulphur, it only seemed to afford the most temporary relief. We simply had to go back to the old and tried expedient of hunting them. We eventually got rid of them the following spring when soap arrived in personal parcels from home and new uniforms from England through the Red Cross, but the ubiquitous lice were certainly one of the discomforts we had to bear that first winter.

During October and November the first letters from home arrived. I was very despondent for a while as the first two or three issues did not include one for me, but at last I got my first letter in November, six months after capture. These letters made a great difference to our lives, and spirits began to rise. In my letter my wife (of five days!) asked me if I could still dance; this seemed a very odd question to ask of anyone in a prisoner-of-war camp, and it was not until after the war that I learned this question had been put in at the request of my mother, who thought it would be a way to find out if I was wounded.

Around this time we also got our first Red Cross parcels. These were intended to be sent and received at the rate of one parcel per man per week, but apparently they were sent by way of Portugal and were held up. According to the griff (i.e. information or rumour) at the time, the Germans were deliberately holding up the Red Cross parcels as they had only 30,000 British prisoners and there was no point in mollycoddling them when they would soon successfully invade Britain and have a million more. I have no idea whether there was any truth in this — certainly I believed it at the time — but for whatever reason the Red Cross parcels sent out from England were not reaching us. At last they came through but initially few and far between. The first issue in Rittel was one parcel for 16 men about six months after capture, and on a similar pattern of one to a number of men now and again for the next few months.

Never mind, they were Red Cross parcels, something rumoured to exist but not to be believed in reality until they actually appeared. The arrival of that first small consignment at Rittel was a great occasion, and the very fact that each parcel had to be divided one to sixteen meant a draw that in itself added to the pleasure of the occasion.

The British Red Cross parcels varied a little in content. They all contained either a tin of stew or bully-beef, a packet of tea, sugar and biscuits, but the other items would vary so that one might get a tin of sardines while another got a packet of Marmite cubes or a similar item supposedly valuable for its vitamins. We were never keen on the vitamin items — solidity was more highly regarded. In those early parcels there was also occasionally a packet of toilet paper. I sometimes wondered whether this had resulted from early letters home, as the lack of toilet paper had been something of a problem to begin with, but now that we had the stuff no one would have dreamed of using it for its normal purpose. Toilet paper was for hoarding against the odd occasion when one might get a screw of tobacco from a Pole and roll a cigarette with it. This did not apply to me for the simple reason that I was quite useless at rolling; whenever I tried to roll a cigarette in this manner the thing fell apart immediately and wasted the tobacco, so I gave it up. Only the early parcels contained this interesting item, and we quite approved of its disappearance as it meant space for another article of food.

November merged into winter, the first of five winters I was to spend in Poland, and easily the worst for all of us. We were constantly hungry and constantly cold. Apart from the issue of a greatcoat, we still had only the clothes in which we had been captured. We were issued with wooden clogs, which were surprisingly warm to the feet in the coldest weather, but swines to march or work in. As socks disintegrated we were also issued with *Füsslappen*, or footrags, little squares of rag to wrap around the feet in place of socks; one had to wrap these as carefully as their small size allowed to both cover the feet and act as a buffer against the chafing of the clogs. We were also issued with what we were given to understand were underpants from Czechoslovakia. These were of woven cotton, coming to well below the knee like a long pair of ladies' knickers, and with tapes at the bottom to tie around the legs. They caused much amusement when they were issued, but we soon learned that they were very practical garments and a lot warmer than the British-issue underpants.

The snow fell and it got colder and yet colder. In January the temperature fell below minus 20°C for the first time and work was stopped. The thermometer continued to fall and one night the guards told us it was 40 below and it was possible to see the frost in the air. The only source of water in the camp was a manual pump which we had sunk ourselves in the summer, and as the water dripped from the spout it froze so that there was a column of ice at all times under the pump.

This was the time of my dream and the frosty bolt. Everyone had dreams of home, more at this time than at any other time in captivity, and I remember my own dream very well. I dreamt one night that I was back in the London streets where I had played as a child, and in particular walking past the local recreation ground known to us kids as 'the Reck'. The war was over and I enjoyed the pleasure of the walk in the spring air, with the flowers blooming in the Reck and remembering my earlier days of captivity, now happily past. But they weren't past. I awoke from this dream to see a bolt which was fastening a roof beam less than a foot above my head, and throughout this winter that bolt was covered with an inch of frost. When people speak of a rude awakening, this is what they mean. The bolt was there, the frost and cold was there, and I was still a prisoner a thousand miles from home.

I dreamt that same dream several times, always, as is the way of dreams, so vividly it must be real, then always awakening to see that thousand-times-accursed bolt. One night I managed something that is so unusual that it must be almost unique. Everyone knows dreams are often so apparently real that in the dream one never queries the reality. One night I had my usual dream and as I walked past the Reck, now back in England with the spring and the flowers and the rest, I reminded myself that this was something I used to dream about years ago when I was in Poland. And as I thought this, I asked myself if I could prove to myself that I was really back, by asking 'How did I return home?' I couldn't answer this, and so told myself I must be dreaming. Then I awoke to the sight of my frost-covered bolt, and was almost pleased this time to have proved to myself I was dreaming. I have never since that single occasion ever had a dream in which I knew I was dreaming.

The cold made spud-bashing an even more unwelcome task than it normally is anyway in the army. The pump worked all right as the water came from a deep well, but it was ice cold, and peeling potatoes in this cold water was less than pleasant. We did this by rotation. There were four huts, each holding about 70 men, and the spud task went round the huts. So did mealtime. With only one issue of soup a day, cooked in one large cauldron, no amount of stirring by the prisoner-cook could alter the fact that the soup drawn from the top was more watery than that at the bottom. We therefore drew soup by rooms in the order 1, 2, 3, 4, and then 2, 3, 4, 1 and so on round the huts.

The visit of a German Medical Officer changed all that, however. He decreed that it was both wasteful and less nutritious to peel spuds, and in future they must be put in the soup in their jackets. This may well have been reasonable in itself, but meant that spud-bashing fatigue would have to wash them thoroughly in icy water instead of peeling them. Inevitably the washing was disposed of as quickly as possible, so that from then on the last hut got even thicker soup than they bargained for; if you were the last you got half a bowl of unsavoury-smelling mud.

Some days were barley days, and there is not a great deal you can do with barley on its own. The cooks were therefore expected to demonstrate their culinary expertise by boiling the stuff until it was as thick as possible, and the first man in the cookhouse that day would emerge with his bowl and the spoon in the bowl — if the spoon stood upright, the cook had done well.

The combination of cold and enforced leisure for a couple of months led me to start a shorthand class. I had been a secretary in London Transport before the war, and in any case my

schooldays were not all that far back, so it was not too difficult to cudgel the mind into remembering the first lessons and
gradual steps of learning. This particular activity is only worth
mentioning for the ingenuity of those soldier-prisoners who
elected to become my pupils. There were of course no textbooks
and teaching had to rely on my memory, but you cannot learn
shorthand by memory. It requires pencil and paper, which we did
not have. We managed to get hold of a couple of pencils which
were handed round, but paper had to be provided by the pupil.
Most achieved this by scrounging empty cigarette packets from
the guards and opening them out, some got labels from used Red
Cross tins, but the way was really shown to all by Sergeant Jim
O'Donnell of the Irish Guards, who was a CID sergeant in Bolton
in pre-war life and determined to take this opportunity to learn
an art useful to a policeman. He got hold of an empty cement
bag, carefully separated its various layers, and made himself a
complete exercise book. Nor was that all. Jim really persevered
and made it worthwhile. During that two months he struggled
with unfamiliar vowel pronunciations (shorthand is phonetic
and the vowel signs are based on which might be called London
English, whereas despite his Irish origins Jim was very much a
Lancastrian in speech, using long vowels where the Southerner
uses short), copied out the day's lesson with no textbook for
reference, and was able to take dictation before spring came and
we went to work again. More will be heard of Jim O'Donnell, a
man of great bravery and determined application to any task he
undertook. I was proud to call him my friend.

Came the spring and work started again. But not for long,
as by early summer I was 'transported' and found myself back
at *Stalag*. Since I had never left it, the phrase 'back at *Stalag*'
requires explanation.

Stalag XXA comprised some 20,000 British prisoners of war, virtually all captured in France or the Low Countries in the battle of France — except for a handful even more unfortunate than the rest of us who were captured a few weeks earlier in Norway. The *Stalag* however was not one large camp. The headquarters was at Thorn in buildings just outside Fort 13, from which most of the prisoner administration staff was drawn — mostly from the QVRs, earning them the label of being 'in the rackets'. Any ex POW will be used to the rackets. The bulk of this large number of prisoners was employed in various working camps in a very wide radius which must have encompassed several hundred square miles. Although the administration staff stayed in Fort 13 for the whole five years, most of us moved around these working camps during the course of our captivity. Any move always entailed going back to Thorn, which was referred to as 'back to *Stalag*', although we had never really left it. We merely moved from one cage to another, and although the Geneva Convention no doubt protected us from some of the horrors of past wars, we were still prisoners.

The Geneva Convention is no doubt an excellent document formulated by well-intentioned men, but the lot of the soldier captured in war by his enemies has not really changed throughout the centuries. He is at the complete mercy of his captors for his form of confinement, his treatment, and literally for every crust of bread to sustain life. In the wars of this twentieth century, civilised nations that are signatories to the Convention may well carry out its provisions, provide medical treatment, permit Red Cross parcels or letters home via the Red Cross and pride themselves that they are more humane than nations in ancient times, but is there really that much difference? Slavery is forbidden by the Convention, but with the exception of the Falklands

War, where both sides were only too glad to send their prisoners back to their homeland as quickly as possible, the prisoners of a modern nation-state in time of war are held in strict confinement and required to work in whatever manner the captors desire. Officers do not work of course under this admirable Convention, but since the bulk of captives in any battle must necessarily be privates and NCOs, this provision can be regarded as no more than a little mutual back-scratching, and a successful battle has exactly the same result for the victors as in Roman or any other times — namely the acquisition of an unpaid labour force. And force it is, since the prisoners are forced to work wherever and at whatever task their captors choose.

Pedants may if they wish point out to me that in modern captivity under the Convention prisoners must be paid, thus avoiding the stigma of slaves. In Germany we got three marks a week, but not in money to spend as a free man may spend: it was in *Lagergeld*, a printed ticket to be worth its face value for spending in the camp canteen. There was no such canteen in any camp I was in, and the pieces of paper had very little value other than as tokens for gambling. As will be seen later, there were occasions where we were able to buy things sometimes, but they were rare and so far as I know most prisoners who held on to their *Lagergeld* brought it back with them five years later. Had I lived in another age and been captured by the Romans there would have been no Convention and I would have been sold into slavery with no nonsense about it. Yet I do not believe there is any record of the Romans or any of the ancient nations confining large numbers of captured prisoners in cages for years on end. Slaves were allowed their freedom within the bond of slavery and from all accounts settled down in a new environment to marry and live a life free of direct confinement. I do not say I would have preferred that, since it is natural for all men to desire to return to their own country, but allowing for the different circumstances of the age, have we really come much further forward?

I have never subscribed to the view that modern war is more terrible than in former times. In the two World Wars of this century machine-guns, high explosives, bombs and the rest have undoubtedly killed on a larger scale than heretofore, but this represents no more than man's eternal inventiveness in finding more efficient ways to kill his fellow humans. I doubt if a soldier in ancient times found it more pleasant to die from a spear in the belly than from a machine-gun burst or shell splinter. The fact is that war is bloody and will never be anything else, but just as the object of war is usually to occupy enemy territory, so the object of battles to attain that end is to kill sufficient of the enemy to encourage the rest to surrender, and this means prisoners *en masse* (nearly two million French soldiers were captured by the Germans in six weeks in the battle of France in 1940). Is there really nothing better to do with them than to put them in cages for years?

Even the Geneva Convention cannot equate humanity with the count of mere numbers of prisoners. In my *Stalag* were soldiers badly wounded in France in 1940 who were not exchanged until 1943, when the British were able to balance the prisoner count after large captures in the western desert.

If civilization has advanced in the past 2000 years, it does not seem to have made exactly giant strides.

March, 1940. Edward and Doris Lyme on their wedding day.

3

The Dolly Mixture

3 1 March 1941 was my first wedding anniversary. On that day in 1940 I had been married with a five-day leave, but as there was no more leave between then and our cross-channel outing to Calais, I had only enjoyed five days of married life. Still there it was, an anniversary, and it called for some sort of celebration.

At that time Denis and I were in Camp 11 A. Two of the forts, 11 and 13, were so full that extra camps were established close by with the fort number and the suffix "A". As far as I know, these camps had only been built in the current and still-young war, but the whole aura of them was of dirt and antiquity, inevitable with the thousands who passed through them in 1940. The accommodation was the same: huge three-tiered shelves for prisoners to lie on cheek by jowl.

On the day of my anniversary the bread ration had been changed to an issue of packets of French hard-tack — the Germans must have captured a mountain of the stuff the previous year. We also had an issue of Red Cross parcels, still very meagre and on the basis of one parcel to a number of men. My prize from this was a half tin of honey, an unusual item in British parcels and the only time I can remember getting it. Good — I would celebrate my wedding date with a cake.

I put the hard-tack on some paper, took off one of my boots, rubbed my hand vaguely across the heel to remove the worst of the mud, and pounded the hard biscuits into crumbs, which assumed a rather dark hue as the particles of earth from my boot joined the mixture. I put this in my bowl, added the honey and some water, and carefully smoothed the top of this now somewhat grey mess to enable me to use my finger to indent the figure 1 on the top. I then put it on the stove until it was almost as hard as the original biscuit. It was disappointing to find that the figure 1 had merely merged with all the other cracks on the top, and I rather wished I had cleaned my boot first, as it could not be denied the thing was a distinctly different colour from the original biscuit. Still it was my personal celebration, and with my next allotted letter I told my wife I had baked a cake for our anniversary. I doubt if the phrase gave her quite the same mental picture as the reality.

Around this time I joined the Padre's religious instruction group. Not, I fear, from a burgeoning of the Holy Spirit, but because the Padre was in Fort 11, and in accordance with the Convention I was entitled to see my spiritual comforter — thus affording a brief opportunity to get out of the camp for a short walk up to the Fort to spend an hour in the Padre's confirmation class. Alas, the man of God was to be disappointed in my case, due to pre-eminence of the stomach over the spirit.

One day, returning to the camp from the Fort, I learned that the Germans were seeking a German speaker for the job of interpreter to the prisoners' detail working in the jerry kitchen, and I promptly applied for the job. In my schooldays, like most boys, I plodded through language sessions and textbooks under sufferance, with neither expectation nor intention of ever doing more than the minimum necessary to avoid the wrath of whatever master was involved, which in my school meant the various masters of Latin, French and Spanish. The Latin master was well-regarded as he made no secret of the fact that he found the subject just as boring as we did, and frequently wandered off into interesting stories of life in the trenches in the First World War. Still, I suppose we absorbed something which probably helped in the French and Spanish classes.

After leaving school I made some effort to learn German at night-school, principally because night-school meant girls and dancing, and one had to take something, but I never got anywhere with German because the construction was so different from the Latin languages. It was not until I met French and other prisoners after my capture at Calais that I found I had a certain facility for languages, and by the time I was in Camp 11A I could cope with German tolerably well. Hence my application for the kitchen job.

The job was not one that would have commended itself to me or anyone else in the normal life of the British Army, being no more than one of the most detested fatigues in military life, namely spud-bashing. At Camp 11A there was a small detail of a half-dozen prisoners who were marched up to the German kitchen each day to peel a mountain of potatoes for the guard company, but this normally hated job took on a most desirable aspect if it was to bring one into proximity with the soup prepared for the guards. Apparently there had been some failure of communication between the Jerry cook-sergeant and the spud-bashing prisoners, so the word was passed for a *Dolmetscher*. The word simply means interpreter in German, but I found that for the rest of my prison camp life I was addressed as much by this title as my own name, although it was of course immediately anglicised to Dolly Mixture or Door-smasher.

There was one small snag before I was able to start. The *Kommandant's* Clerk sent for me to tell me that the Padre had protested strongly against the loss of one of his prisoners half-way through confirmation class, and demanded my return for further religious instruction. I protested equally strongly that I was the best judge of the comparative worth of my future hopes of a halo and the present possibility of an extra bowl of soup. The soup won by several lengths, and I joined the kitchen detail.

The kitchen fatigue lasted a couple of months and was quite a pleasant time. We were a chummy little group, marching off to the guard cook-house each day and spending our day sitting around a large tub of water gradually filling it up with peeled spuds, recounting to each other our personal lives in a faded past and another world, with a bowl of Jerry soup at the end of it. This personal baring of souls was no more than a pleasant change of subject from the three standard ingredients of all prison camp discussions throughout the whole war. One is obvious, and the other two were food and the state of the war, all three as natural a part of our daily lives as breathing. Not for us the academic interest in the state of the war of a free public back home. Assuming we were going to win— and nobody ever assumed anything else — it was important to us to know when we were going to stop back-pedalling and start moving forward.

The first and standard subject, although constant, carried less widespread experience from young men raised in the 1930s than would be the case today, and the modern teenager might be at least a little surprised and probably contemptuous at the lack of depth in our exchanges. On the other hand, in five years of captivity in conditions where one might expect homosexuality to flourish, it was, if not unknown, at the least very rare. In all that time and in different camps I only knew of one case for certain and a couple of presumed cases. No doubt it would be greatly different today.

One day the Jerry cook took me on a tour of his store to ask me the English names for the various vegetables. The main vegetable room was quite artistic, having a well-executed mural on the wall depicting a German soldier on a park bench with a girl on his knee and his hand up her skirt. In one corner of this room was a large pile of what I took to be parsnips, although he said the German name was *Sellerie*. I said we had a celery also, but it was quite different and these articles were parsnips. I remember he got me to pronounce it carefully in two syllables, par-snips, so that he could remember it. Later we got some of these items cut up, and to my surprise they proved to be celery after all — it appears the Germans use the root for flavouring soups, whereas we use the stem. These roots looked to me just like parsnips, so there may be a German somewhere to this day who thinks the English word for celery is 'parsnip'.

After a couple of months at this kitchen I found myself transferred more or less round the corner to camp 13A, next to Fort 13, which was the hub of the whole Stalag. My abode of bliss in this camp was the Black Hut.

Camp 13A, like all the others, had a number of huts, all containing the three-tiered shelves as mass bunks, and all dirty, but none so black with accumulated filth as the Black Hut. It was swept each day by prisoners with birch-twig besoms, but shelves, floor, tables, benches and anything else in the hut remained a standard black.

From here I found myself on a working party, marching only a mile or two in the vicinity to dig narrow, shallow trenches. It was quite easy to work out their purpose. Unless we were much mistaken, these trenches were to be filled in due course with cement to form the foundations of huts just like the Black Hut, and if this judgement was anywhere near the mark, it looked as though we were preparing the basis of a very large prison camp. This seemed to be confirmed when the German sergeant in charge of the work came to me one day and asked me to ask the others to be good chaps and do him a favour by filling in one of the trenches we had only just dug and digging some more on the opposite side. He showed me his plan — the silly bugger had marked out the ground with the plan upside-down.

But a prison camp for whom? The Germans were not currently in contact with British troops, and their allies the Italians were surrendering in large numbers in the desert rather than capturing British soldiers. So why this new prison camp? Could it possibly be in readiness for a war with Russia?

We discussed this but found it impossible to accept. Not only did Germany have a nonaggression pact with Russia (the original cause of our own captivity in fact), but if the tales we had heard about the size of the Red Army were anywhere near true it seemed unlikely that even Hitler would stick his neck out that far.

Nevertheless, there we were undoubtedly preparing foundations for huts in a pattern with which we were only too familiar. They must be intended for someone, and had to be taken in conjunction with obvious troop movements. During winter, all German troop movements appeared to be eastwards. That continued. Not so much at first, but gradually increasing, so that by the summer of 1941 each day saw more conveys moving east. As we were in Poland, and that land was divided between Russians and Germans following the mutually agreed partition after the

German/Polish war, the eastern frontier was fairly close to our camp complex. This made the troop movements seem sensible and nonsensical at the same time. If Hitler really intended to attack Russia, he was certainly concentrating a hell of a powerful army to do it. But at the same time, knowing we were not all that far from the frontier ourselves, it just did not seem possible that all these troops could be concentrated between us and the border without the Russians knowing it. Still, there it was, a stream every day of tanks, lorries, half-tracks, guns, the lot, all moving eastwards.

Despite the evidence of our own eyes, despite the constant speculation, it was a surprise when it came. On 22 June 1941 we were on *Appel* (roll-call) when the word went round. We heard no guns, the guards said nothing, but the word went round. He's done it. The stupid bastard's attacked Russia.

We were quite pleased with this. We knew the power of the *Wehrmacht*, we had been on the wrong end of it ourselves, and had seen this huge machine moving up to the start line for months. But anything that occupied the German Army must, in our view, be to our advantage in hastening the end of the war. And in this case surely he had bitten off more than he could chew?

Yet common sense said the Germans would not have started a war with Russia unless they expected to win it, and there was the camp we had helped to prepare, presumably one of many. We they really that confident? They were, and confidence seemed be justified. Each day came the news that the *Wehrmacht* was advancing further into Russia, and apparently at high speed. Their successes could hardly be denied when we saw the long column of Russian prisoners arriving in the *Stalag* area, and a sorry sight they looked, too. They had clearly suffered great privation in their initial stages of captivity, and were to continue to do so. For some time that summer those of us who were working in the area of the Russian camp got used to seeing the death cart each afternoon taking the bodies of dead Russian prisoners to a mass grave.

By contrast, my own fortunes as a prisoner of war were about to improve considerably. In July 1941 I found myself part of working party of 350 marched off to a new camp only a few miles from the central *Stalag* at Thorn. This camp appeared to completely isolated, and I never saw any village or township nearby from which the camp may have taken its name, but it had a name, and one not forgotten by any prisoner who lived in it over the year of 1941/1942 — Schlüsselmühle.

4

Red Cross Parcels and Red Cross Trains

Schlüsselmühle was approached by a dusty road through a barren area of sand, like a miniature version of the Sahara desert, and had the same 'Abandon All Hope' appearance of any prison camp — the usual barbed-wire perimeter, barbed-wire gates, guards, *Kommandantur* huts outside and, as seen by an entering prisoner, a *deja vu* air of merely moving from one prison to another.

But this one was different inside. This was more like it. The accommodation would be regarded by anyone living a normal life as spartan in the extreme, consisting of blocks of huts with each room containing wooden bunks and a total furniture of one table with a form each side. But a prisoner of war is not living a normal life, and comfort is comparative. To those of us who had been in the Black Hut the difference was dazzling.

To start with, these huts were clean, with room for 12 men in a room, and one-up, one-down wooden bunks, the first time for many of us that we had slept solo since capture more than a year ago. The tables were clean (and we kept them that way), there was a washhouse hut, a *Revier* (the German word for sick-bay, and never called anything else but The Revier), and even a recreation hut with a platform for a stage.

Since the Germans selected these working parties simply by an assembly of prisoner of war numbers, it was quite common to find pretty well everyone a stranger to everyone else; it didn't matter very much as it was a type of life where one quickly paired off with a kindred soul as a 'mucker'. 'Mucking-in' was the term automatically applied to any two friends who worked together and shared everything, and the majority of prisoners mucked in with someone else. Sometimes there were more than two, but two was most common.

I had been parted from Denis for some time now, although I was to meet him again at a later camp, and found myself two new friends to form a trio to muck in - Douglas and Basil. I cannot remember their surnames, and possibly did not know them, as surnames were seldom used anyway. We got along very well together, although why they suffered me I really do not know; I didn't pull my weight in the trio, although in self-justice I tried to do so. When we had Red Cross parcels, it was Doug who was always up before I was awake and gave Basil and me a mug of tea in bed (!), and when there was cooking to do it was always either Basil or Doug who did it. I did the washing up.

The up-market accommodation in Schlüsselmühle was not the only improvement in our lot that summer. Starting in the autumn of the previous year we had received Red Cross parcels, but in such small numbers that we had to draw lots for each item. This had persisted until almost the time of our transfer to Schlüsselmühle, but we had scarcely settled in when the contents of cornucopia were poured upon us. It seemed Red Cross parcels had been sent from England at the rate of one a week per man, but as we had clearly not been getting them, a huge stock had built up somewhere - we always understood this stock was in Lisbon whither it had been sent from England for transfer to Germany. Be that as it may, the floodgates were suddenly opened, and for a glorious period of a couple of months at Schlüsselmühle we got two parcels per man every ten days. Once the stock was exhausted nothing like it ever happened again, but for a short period food was abundant.

Schüsselmüle, 1941. With Doug.

The up-market accommodation in Schlüsselmühle was not the only improvement in our lot that summer. Starting in the autumn of the previous year we had received Red Cross parcels, but in such small numbers that we had to draw lots for each item. This had persisted until almost the time of our transfer to

Schlüsselmühle, but we had scarcely settled in when the contents of a cornucopia were poured upon us. It seemed Red Cross parcels had been sent from England at the rate of one a week per man, but as we had clearly not been getting them, a huge stock had built up somewhere (we always understood this stock was in Lisbon whither it had been sent from England for transfer to Germany). Be that as it may, the floodgates were suddenly opened, and for a glorious period of a couple of months at Schlüsselmühle we got two parcels per man every ten days. Once the stock was exhausted nothing like it ever happened again, but for a short period food was abundant.

Nor was this all. The British Army had sent out new uniforms and underclothing for all, and we were not only issued with new uniforms but with British greatcoats and boots. Soap had already arrived in personal parcels, and it is impossible to exaggerate the lifting of spirits which came with a recovery of self-respect. We were soldiers again, and although there were still to be other times of privation, we never again sank to the depths of the first year.

In addition to the Red Cross parcel issue, we were entitled by Geneva Convention to receive three personal parcels from home per year. These were limited to 11 lb in weight, and to consist solely of underclothing, socks, pullovers and the like for personal use. In Schlüsselmühle we wore these items (in any case we badly needed the underwear), but in later camps where there was contact with the Poles, the socks and the pullovers were promptly flogged for eggs. There was a regular *bourse* in this — eggs being at the rate of three or four for a pair of socks, and between 20 and 30 for a pullover. The only items other than clothing allowed in these parcels were a single bar of soap and a single bar of chocolate. The chocolate always tasted of soap, even when it was packed on the opposite side to the soap.

Schlüsselmühle, 1941.

We were soon sent out to work in parties labelled by letters of the alphabet. I was in M gang, and M gang was concerned with shifting large quantities of sand. Whatever they wanted the stuff for there was certainly no shortage of it. Sand was all around us, like sea-water to the Ancient Mariner, and just as inexhaustible.

We did not have to dig the stuff ourselves. There was a huge sand dredger mounted on a track about eight feet wide. This was, in German, the *Bagger* and as the German 'a' is pronounced like an 'uh', this was at least one article where everyone had perfect Teutonic pronunciation. The Bagger moved slowly along its track digging out sand and depositing it in skips drawn by a light engine on a two-foot gauge railway. When the Bagger had moved to the end of its track, our job was to slew the lines over another few feet so that the Bagger could move slowly back on its track with fresh sand to dig. We spent months doing nothing else each day but move the track after the Bagger had passed, then go behind it and start all over again.

The slewing was done simply by each man taking a long metal pole, sticking it under the track, and the whole gang heaving in unison. At first the *Eingedeutsched* Pole — a Pole who had thrown in his lot with the Germans (there were comparatively few, as the Poles are fiercely patriotic) — who was the *Meister*, or Foreman, on the job, stood on the sleepers and called out appropriate monosyllables which would presumably have sounded just right if the gang had been German or Polish, but he soon found out the British heaved better with one of their own number calling out in English. This was clearly a job just made for me, and I gave up my pole and spent my days calling 'Ho...Hup', while standing on the sleepers and being heaved across with the rails. This was certainly a lot better than heaving those bloody rails all day, but is not quite as column-dodging as it sounds. We preferred one of our own number, and obviously I could not have simply given myself the job unless it had been generally agreed as to who should do it. Several others had a go at it at one time or another, but it always came back to me. I was pretty skinny in those days, and not only light to stand on the rails, but no great loss of heaving power to the rest of the gang. And there was no doubt we worked a lot better that way than with the *Meister*. It gradually came to mean that M gang finished a bit earlier than the others.

After only 15 months' captivity we had already got to the stage of calling the camp 'home' and when the day's work was finished, spoke of 'going home'. God help us.

All the mountains of sand we were seeing off in the light

railways were only moved a mile or so away and dumped where other gangs were working. In addition to the British prisoners there were a thousand or so Poles and a large number of German technicians working on what was at that time a huge barren site. In M gang we saw nothing of this hive of activity, being remote in our own desert, but it soon transpired that the whole workforce — probably numbering 2000 in all — was engaged in the initial stages of preparing a site for the establishment of a railway siding complex and a large locomotive shed a few miles outside the main railway station at Thorn.

We were not greatly interested in what they did with the sand or what they were building. Now that we had Red Cross parcels and clean clothing, the minds of some of us turned to some form of recreation.

A concert party! We would have a concert party.

We already had a stage in the as yet unused recreation hut, and once the word went round the enthusiasm was great. Necessity is supposed to be the mother of invention, and certainly in this case apparently insurmountable obstacles were not only overcome, but easily so. Curtains were easy, by the sacrifice of blankets. Wings, and in due course furniture, were made from Red Cross wooden cases scrounged from Central *Stalag*. Lighting was of course fixed by experts — we had experts in almost everything in the camp (in *Stalag* they were already assembling a cadre of forgers for the provision of identity cards for escapers) — backdrops were painted with coloured powder, and ladies' dresses made in the early shows from paper, but later from bits and pieces which produced remarkable clothing, from a nurse's outfits to a long evening dress.

Camp Concert 1942. The dresses were made from paper and the props from Red Cross boxes. The background drops were painted with coloured powder. The author is the schoolmaster here, in a Will Hay sketch.

During the 15 months I was at Schlüsselmühle we progressed from fairly simple variety shows to full musicals and serious drama. The Germans became so interested they took photographs, and I have some of these to this day, as well as the programmes. The programmes also progressed, being at first simply written by hand, and eventually, by dint of a little bribery and corruption, passed by guards to the local newspaper office in Thorn and printed. They were of course no more than simple fold-over programmes, but printed nevertheless, and I still have the programmes for *Tit Bits* (variety), *Idyll Moments* (a full scale musical which I had written plagiarising the Eddie Cantor film *Roman Scandals*, but with the venue moved from Rome to Ancient Egypt, in which I enjoyed myself no end as a wicked High Priest), and — what was for me the highlight of our concert party in Schlüsselmühle — *The Amazing Dr Clitterhouse*, a very well-known pre-war play by Barré Lyndon.

'The Amazing Dr Clitterhouse'

Clitterhouse had a remarkable sequel more than a generation later. The play had a large cast, with two female parts. One was played by Ken Gowing, who was a first-class female impersonator, and for the other, a character called Nurse Ann, we found a new 'actress', one Jim Allen. I was playing *Clitterhouse*, and Jim was my nurse/receptionist. The play was a great success in the camp, but like the concert party itself and everything else at

Schlüsselmühle (including the abundance of Red Cross parcels), it faded into the past as we moved on and the war itself dragged on for another three years. Thirty-eight years later, in 1980, I went to the telephone one day to hear a very deep male voice say 'This is Nurse Ann.' Astonishingly my mind clicked into the right place at once. It was indeed Jim Allen, and he lived in the next village. He had seen my name in the local newspaper, phoned them, and they put him in touch. Later the same newspaper presented us with a bottle of champagne, and gave us a front page photograph of our reunion.

Another constant member of the concert party was Johnny Wise, and he and I had something of a rapport on the stage. For one show we had a sketch in which we were supposed to be a couple of cowboys, and at one point Johnny referred to some unseen cowboys as coming from the Bar X ranch. Johnny, on the spur of the moment, called it the Lazy M and brought the house down. At that time, by chance rather than arrangement, more than half the concert party was on M gang, shifting rails and getting in a bit earlier than the others. From that time onwards we were the Lazy M.

M gang worked in a sea of sand, the only signs of human civilisation being the camp itself about a mile away, a railway line a few hundred yards beyond the Bagger, a small hut where we could sit for our mid-day break, and of course the small one-man wooden privy common to all building sites everywhere. I dare say the Egyptians had one when they were building the pyramids.

This latter article of necessity was simply placed over a deep hole dug in the sand, and when the hole was full we just dug another hole a few yards away, picked up the privy, moved it to the new position, and flung some sand over the old hole. It afforded great satisfaction to all one day when the *Meister* walked over the thin covering on the previous hole and sank in to his thighs. He could not go home to change without dismissing his workforce of prisoners, and even in the wide open air of our desert he stank abominably. But we finished early that day.

It was with M gang on my birthday that I came the closest I ever got to the little bastard Adolf himself. On 29 August 1941 we marched out to the Bagger site as usual and knew immediately some event was expected, which was clearly connected with the railway line about a quarter of a mile away. German soldiers were spaced along the whole line at around 200-yard intervals, with an extra guard on the one small bridge that was within our vision. Since this line went to Berlin one way and to somewhere in Russia the other, many thousands of troops must have been involved in merely standing beside the railway track. For some time that morning our own guards, rather stupidly, tried to pretend there was nothing unusual going on; but eventually, long after we had worked it out for ourselves, they told us Hitler was to pass that way to visit the Russian front.

Our two guards must have had some strict orders that day as they displayed unwonted diligence in watching us, although it was difficult to see what damage would be offered to the beloved Fuhrer by unarmed prisoners some distance from a railway line along which a train would pass at speed and with half the German Army in the way. No chances were taken, and at around noon we were herded into the site hut, the solitary window was covered up, the door shut, and we were ordered not to look out on pain of being promptly shot.

Even in our daily break time we did not normally all go into the hut together as it was too small, and with all of us in there it was packed tight. I was up against the wall facing the railway line, and through a knot-hole I could see quite clearly. At around one o'clock that day the guards on the line stiffened to attention and a train steamed along eastwards at high speed. The Fuhrer obviously protected his health with some care. The train was quite short, consisting of the engine with tender, an armoured box-car presumably containing troops, another box-car, and another armoured car. Our Adolf made sure he was All Right Jack. Or perhaps he felt there were some people who didn't like him.

The railway line was a natural source of interest for us, and we got to know and to time the local passenger trains and the Europa Express to Berlin. These were interspersed with troop movements and other war traffic; one type of train in particular gave a grim comment on the progress of the war on the Eastern Front and, even at the time of shattering German successes, must have been sobering at whatever point the trains were received. It was the Red Cross train.

At first all the war traffic seemed to be one way, tanks, guns, troops, all being carried to the east, with just an occasional train with broken tanks or a Red Cross train going the other way. Then as summer merged into autumn and Russian resistance began to tell, the Red Cross trains increased. These obviously contained men wounded in battle, but it was in the winter of 1941/2 that the toll of the Eastern Front on the German Army really began to show.

The Red Cross trains increased from 'occasionally' to two or three a week, then to one a day, and then to several in a day. These carried not wounded, except in the technical sense of wounds on active service — they were frostbite cases. The winter of 1940/1 had been one of the severest Europe had known for many years, and Heaven knows we had suffered enough from that in the camp at Rittel and elsewhere in the *Stalag*. Winter 1941/2 was equally cold, but this time we had better camp conditions, warm

British greatcoats and above all better food from the Red Cross parcels. In short, we were better equipped, but exactly the opposite applied to the German troops on the Russian Front. It is well known that Hitler sent his army into Russia with the expectation of a complete victory before winter, and the troops had no winter clothing. Many units had little more than the summer uniforms they stood up in, and in a much greater cold than we were experiencing in Poland (bad enough for us, at sometimes around 20°C below), were suffering agonies of intense cold, leading in many cases to severe frostbite.

If we saw two or three Red Cross trains during the day, it could presumably be reckoned that there were another couple in the night, and this line was only one of a half-dozen lines leading from Germany into Russia. The Germans suffered over half a million casualties from the fighting — Adolf's eastern venture was costing his countrymen dear.

Most the chaps called these Red Cross trains the meat train, but although I rejoiced as much as anyone in German casualties — each of which must be counted as a step towards the end of the war — I could not joke about these Red Cross trains. I remembered only two well (and still do) my utter misery the previous winter, and felt sorry for the poor sods. This did not alter my joy at the increase of these trains; the more killed and injured, the better our chances of an end to our own incarceration. Does all this sound contradictory? What else is war?

Christmas came and went — a much better Christmas than the previous one at Rittel where conditions, food and clothing were all at their nadir. This time we had Red Cross food parcels, warm clothing and clean conditions, and we held a Christmas party in my room with invitations to another room to share. The following week that room invited us back to share with them for a New Year's party, the only time I can remember in that long captivity when there was enough food to play host to someone else.

As we moved into spring a change came over our work. Enough sand had been moved to the sidings site to cause the demise of M gang, and we moved to join other gangs working on the main site. This was a huge area, with each gang wrapped up in its own business. It was around this time that *Akkord Arbeit* came into its own.

Arbeit simply means work, and the word was so universal in Germany that it was used by prisoners of various nationalities more than the equivalent word in their own languages. *Akkord* was something new and I never knew it to apply to anyone other than the British in Schlüsselmühle.

It meant task work, and represented a late awakening on the part of our captors to the notion that British prisoners were quite capable of working 15 hours a day without producing any noticeable result, but given a specific task with the promise of a return to home ('home' — again, God help us!) they would complete the task in half the time the Poles would take.

This meant the day's work started with negotiations between the gang and the *Meister* as to the number of mixings of cement or the size of the hole to be dug for that day's *Akkord*, and I found myself not only unofficial interpreter but unofficial shop steward as well. No matter what the task for the day, there was always at least one man on the gang, frequently several, who was used to that particular job in civvy street, and could state fairly accurately what was reasonable for the day. I got fairly professional at these assessments myself, and rather enjoyed the morning's initial bargaining with the *Meister*. After all, I had to mix the cement or dig the bloody hole myself as well. We had an official 12-hour day, and most gangs negotiated a day's work on the basis that if it could not be done in six hours, we would refuse the task and work the whole 12 hours, when the *Meister* would know very well that practically no work would be done at all. The guards usually supported us in this, as a successful *Akkord* meant they reduced their duty time by several hours. Though not always. Sometimes if we got too bolshie, the guard would support the *Meister*, and then we would work 12 hours; he might even take his rifle off his shoulder and we would have to work hard as well. We were still prisoners.

Generally however the *Akkord* idea worked well to the satisfaction of both sides, and once the task had been accepted the prisoners really worked hard to get the job done and return 'home'. There was a notable occasion when one of the German soldiers, guarding a gang of the night shift, collapsed during the shift. The night's *Akkord* having been accepted, and the gang already working like fury to get it over, the guard was simply laid out in the gang's hut until the task was over, then the gang returned to the camp on their own carrying the guard between them.

When I was working on the cement-mixing gang, I found it such hard work that I wished we had a cement mixer to do the job. Then we got one, and I regretted my wish, since of course we then had to work harder to keep up with the mixer. It was on this job one day that I idly let my shovel clatter over the rivets on the cement mixer, like a child rattling a stick against the railings. Unfortunately the end of the shovel caught in one of the rivets and the hand end shot back and forth like a piston deep into my stomach. This time it was I who was carried back to the camp and put to bed in the Revier.

Schlüsselmühle was large enough to have a British medical officer, and the Revier was in the charge of Colonel McCarthy, RAMC. He was a good officer and a good doctor, but led a rather remote life as the only officer in the camp. He diagnosed nothing more than internal bruising requiring a couple of weeks' rest in the Revier, which strangely enough was not as welcome as one might think. It was far better to be out with my friends than stuck in bed in the Revier, but there I was and I had to stay there a fortnight. We were short of books, and in the Revier I found a German school primer on Italian. I idly started to read this and to attempt to follow the Italian via the German, and became sufficiently interested to keep on with it after I left the Revier. In 1943/44 it became possible to take Royal Society of Arts examinations in the prison camp, and I eventually passed one of these in Italian, stemming solely from my sick-bay German primer. I do not mention this from any personal boasting, as I have forgotten it all by this time anyway, but as an instance of the concentration of mind forced on a prisoner with no normal outlet for mental energy or recreation. Alexandre Dumas gives an excellent example of this in the Abbé Faria character in *The Count of Monte Cristo*.

My initial muckers in Schlüsselmühle, Doug and Basil, had gone back to Stalag, and I was now mucking in with George Sketchley, a bank clerk in that private life before the war which we referred to as 'real life'. George was a wonderful and staunch friend, and we were good muckers for the rest of the Schlüsselmühle stint.

When I returned to the working site, it was evidently felt by the *Meister*, known as Joseph, that I was best kept away from the cement mixer in case I did the same thing to anyone else (not unjustified, I was a careless worker) and he gave me a job with another chap bending iron rods. This was to prove disastrous to him. If the phrase on the cigarette packets had been thought of then, I am sure I should have worn a label saying that contact with me could prove dangerous to health.

Most of the workers, prisoners and Poles, were concentrated round the now rising loco shed, but my gang was some distance away in what was to be the sidings area. As this was soft sand, it needed reinforcing by driving huge concrete piles into the ground. But first the piles had to be made and required their own steel cage or reinforcement inside. This cage was made of four very long steel rods bound together with a lattice work of wire. The rods had to be bent over at one end into a U shape, and this job was given to my friend and me. It was the *Meister's* undoing.

The job was simple enough. All we had to do was to lay a rod on a very long table with one end protruding and held firm by metal lugs on the table. Then we took a hollow steel bar, inserted one end of it in the rod and walked round in a semicircle, thus bending the end of the rod. Simplicity itself, what could go wrong?

The fact is that nothing should have gone wrong, and we were quite happy in a pleasant non-arduous task in the summer sun, quietly bending our rods, when Joseph visited us and said we could work twice as fast by putting two rods in at the same time.

We protested that the lugs on the table would not hold two rods at the same time, and even if they did it would be too much to bend at one time. Joseph proved we were wrong on the first count by putting two rods in the lugs and holding them there, so we inserted our bar and ostensibly strained to walk round without apparent being able to move. We were of course only registering a standard protest, and could have bent two rods as easily as one, but objection to any increase of work was quite automatic.

Joseph now held the rods in place and told us to push harder. In order to show what a great effort was required, we made a snatching run at the bar. Joseph cried out and ran off. We look at the rods where they were held by the lugs and saw something which should not have been there. I put my hand in and picked out Joseph's thumb.

Joseph was not a popular *Meister*, and when the word went round, as it did quickly, we two were subject to some cheerful banter for having done a good job. We did not feel that way however; we were truly contrite and wanted to let Joseph know an ambulance had been sent for, and meantime Joseph was in the *Meister's* cabin. I therefore went in on behalf of the two of us to express our apologies.

I had to admire Joseph for his toughness. He was sitting at a table eating his dinner soup with the spoon in his right hand, holding his left hand away from the soup with blood-soaked cottonwool round the base of his missing thumb, still welling blood strongly. In answer to my shame-faced apology, he just pointed with his spoon to the damage, and with his mouth full of potato told me to be more careful in future.

I was not finished with my disasters on this job. If someone had had the sense to send a report of my work to the Fuhrer, I am sure he would either have sent me home or had me shot out of the way. I simply did not further the war economy of the Third Reich.

The cages of reinforcement (made by someone else after Joseph's little misfortune) were placed in long troughs, filled with cement, and in due course became concrete piles 60 feet long, ready for lifting and placing in preparation for the pile-driver.

For the lifting part of it there was a huge crane which strad-dled the piles like a cage, with two sets of hooks that hooked into iron lugs left in the concrete and thus lifted the pile out of the trough. This crane was operated by electricity and a simple set of switches. Joseph was back on the job and worked the crane himself. He only had to press the right buttons and the crane did the work, but he was always careful in lifting the pile out of the trough, as concrete that had spilled from the neighbouring piles had to be broken off by gently lifting each pile an inch or two at a time until it was freed from its fellow. All went well until Joseph, who should have known better, told me to work the crane one day.

I rather fancied myself as a crane driver; this would be just my cup of tea. Watched by Joseph, I correctly pressed the right switches to manoeuvre the crane over the spread of concrete piles, and then to lower the two hooks down to the nearest pile. This was where I made my mistake. I should have gently eased the pile up clear of the others. Instead I just checked the pile was hooked on and pressed hard on the raising button. It all happened too quickly for Joseph to intervene. The pile was held to the rest on either side by spilled concrete in the centre. The crane strained, the pile — reinforced concrete — bent like a bow, and then snapped back straight with a loud crack from the crane's electricity box, and the crane wires snaking off their pulleys to the ground.

Feelings were mixed about me that day. The camp in general, when they heard of it, approved this destruction of an enemy crane. My own gang was not so pleased, as they made us work that day till three in the morning; although little work was done it was a damn nuisance when we had got used to finishing early. It took a week to repair that crane. My friends just waited with interest to see when my worth as a construction worker would be further demonstrated. They had not long to wait.

The next step in this job sequence was for the pile-driver to drive these long piles into the sand for the whole of their 60-foot length. We were then required to dig a trench six feet deep and wide enough to cover the area of the now sunken piles, so that when the trench was completed the tops of the piles now protruded from the floor of the trench like sticks of asparagus.

The next and last step was to bend the tops of the piles below the original surface of the sand so that they would form a strong basis for a concrete platform. Since one cannot bend concrete this meant breaking off the top six feet of the pile and bending the inner rod-and-wire cage. For this purpose I was sent off to the stores for a couple of *Lufthammers*.

I was frequently faced with some German word I had not come across before, but usually the context of the sentence told me the meaning. When I was really stumped, I found it embarrassing. I was supposed to be able to speak German, and it was awkward when I didn't know and had no one to ask.

What on earth was a *Lufthammer*, literally an airhammer? I must have been in a dim mood that day, as it should have been obvious, but I went off to the stores struggling in my mind to envisage some type of hammer you hit air with. I was given two large pneumatic drills, which I could hardly carry back to the site.

We were supposed to have been issued with small hand drills, but apparently they were not available at the moment, so we had two full-size drills, which meant one man holding the end against the concrete horizontally, while the other worked the drill. It was arduous, uncomfortable, and if the drill slipped, damned dangerous. On the whole, though, we liked it — it was more interesting than mixing concrete.

Eventually we got the hand drills, and the very first time

I used one I handled it carelessly and the point slipped off the concrete pile. This meant the steel drill shot off the tool, and with the pneumatic power behind it, whooshed past the rest of the gang like a bolt from a crossbow, buried itself in the ground about three feet down and had to be dug out. Thereafter, and with good-fellowship and perfect understanding all round, the gang worked at one end of the trench and I worked at the other end.

We were getting near the end of our time in Schlüsselmühle, but I cannot leave without mentioning the fleas. In the late summer of 1942 we were visited by a plague of fleas. They were sand fleas and not confined to the camp, but we seemed to get more of them in the camp, and there were evenings when sections of the ground outside the huts were literally alive with them, looking like a black cloud hovering over the earth. They were a damn nuisance, we were all badly bitten — and I wrote home asking if it was possible to send some Keatings Powder in the next parcel. That must have given them something to think about. After the war my wife showed me a letter from the Red Cross regretting they could not put this article in a parcel.

Eventually, like all things, the plague ended, and so did our time at Schlüsselmühle. George and I went back to *Stalag*, where we continued to muck in together in Fort 13.

Fort 13 contained about 1500 prisoners, more than half of whom were permanently domiciled there as headquarters staff in the administration block just down the road. The rest were transient, just in *Stalag* for a short period between transports or working parties. The transient men usually hated the place, but everything is relative, and the staff men seemed to like their surroundings as they were well settled in.

One day I was in my room in *Stalag* (still with the three-tiered shelves for sleeping) when a very large man came in. He was an Inniskilling — a member of the Inniskilling regiment — over six feet in height, and a very powerful man in body. He said he had been on a job where the work was so hard and the food so poor he finally had to 'go sick', although he normally liked hard work. This one had been just too much. Then he asked if there was a feller named Lyme in this room. I acknowledged my name and he came over and looked me up and down.

'You poor sod,' said this encouraging gentleman. 'You're my replacement on the worst farm in all Germany. It'll kill you.'

5

A Slice off a Cut Loaf

The Schmidt's farm was not the worst in Germany – I was to find a worse one on my very next transport — but it was certainly the worst in the village, and regarded as such by everyone, Germans and Poles alike.

Farm work was highly regarded in *Stalag*, and most prisoners were anxious to get onto one. There were certainly stories of large farms where the work was long and arduous with no redeeming features, but there were also accounts of small farms with only one prisoner, no guards, and good living with willing Polish young women as work mates. I remember one chap returning to *Stalag* and making us all jealous with his stories of so many chicken meals he had got tired of chicken, and accounts of his frequent tumbles with Polish girls in the hay. I didn't fancy agricultural work too much, but the rest of it sounded acceptable enough.

It's all the luck of the draw, and I was unlucky to be dealt the only losing number out of ten — the other nine were winners.

The camp was the smallest I was ever in; there were just ten men, including me as a replacement, housed in one end of a barn which had been converted to house them. There were the usual up-and-down bunks, a table and forms, and outside the door a simple barbed-wire fence only a few feet from the side of the barn, offering minimal exercise space. Not that it mattered since no one was likely to want exercise after a day's work on a farm. There was only one guard, and each morning he just unlocked the door and each prisoner went out on his own to his own farm, worked for the day, and came back on his own. They all appeared to be quite satisfied with the form of life here, as they all had good farms and food. Except, that is, for my predecessor, and now me.

The Schmidts were Bessarabians; it is long forgotten now, and was already fading into the past then, that when Hitler attacked Poland, secure in his non-aggression pact with Stalin, the Russians occupied half of Poland, but also took the opportunity to grab a slice of Bessarabia. No one could do much about it, and the Bessarabians, who were almost all farmers, were re-settled by the Nazis by the simple expedient of giving them farms in Poland.

The Schmidt farm was, I suppose, no different from the others, and Herr Schmidt was not a bad chap. The trouble was that he was married to Frau Schmidt.

Schmidt was a huge man, taller than me, and I am 6 feet; but whereas I was as thin as the proverbial rake, he was wide-shouldered, large and powerful. In almost comic cartoon contrast, his wife was small and thin, but what a virago! She ruled her husband, the Polish hands, and, I gathered, the village as well when she had the chance. I don't think that would have mattered to me, since she was in no position to rule a prisoner of war, but with it she was miserly and mean to the last degree.

There were two Polish hands, Lena and Stanislaus. Lena was about 20, and there would normally have been no reason why she and I could not make music together. But Frau Schmidt watched over her like a duenna when I was around, although it had nothing to do with her. Stan was an experienced farm hand and dealt mostly with the livestock; the farm had arable land growing both potatoes and grain, and some pasture land for a small herd of cows. There were also a couple of horses for the plough.

The food was terrible with no excuse for it on a farm. There was no question of eating with the family on this farm; the Schmidts ate in the kitchen, and Lena, Stan and I in the tiny scullery. I don't know what the Schmidts ate, but the soup they gave us was awful. I learned that my predecessor had no German at all, which was unusual for the general run of prisoners by this time, and when the soup was just too bad for him he could only show his feelings by throwing it out of the door. It was really shortsighted of Frau Schmidt to have treated my Iniiskilling friend in this way, as in the short time we had spoken together in Stalag he told me he was a farmworker in civilian life, and as he was a powerful man, a little reasonable treatment of him would have given the Schmidts a good prisoner-of-war farmhand. Instead he 'went sick' and they got me. Served them right.

I was a townie, a Londoner, and had never been on a farm before. My capabilities as an agricultural worker proved to be well down to the standard I had already attained as a construction worker, with the marginal possibility of being even worse.

I was at least lucky in one way. I was only on this farm for two months in October/November 1942, and by the time I arrived most of the back-breaking toil was over. The spuds had been lifted and most of the threshing done, so that most of the time it was a question of finding work for me to do.

The first job was a spot of ploughing. Schmidt took me with a single horse and plough to a field, and went round the field a couple of times; he did not plough up and down but in concentric squares so that he would eventually finish in the middle of the field. After a couple of squares, he handed me the reins and told me to get on with it and finish the field. Then he just turned his back and walked back to the farm.

What the hell was I to do? The horse looked placid enough, but it was certainly larger than me; was it safe? Did it have enough intelligence to know where to go, as I had no idea of how to turn it at the corners? Oh well, one must make a start. But it didn't start. The stupid animal didn't understand English, and my 'Ho Hups' got nowhere. I tried copying the sounds the farmer had made — something like a 'Hee Haw Hick' — and the beast started off. I soon found it easy enough to turn the corners with a pull on the reins, but when I wanted to stop my 'Whoas' were wasted. This one at least I knew, as I had heard Poles stop their horses on the road at Rittel. One pretended it was freezing and said 'Brrrr'. It worked perfectly. I learned very little Polish in Poland (German was the *lingua franca*) but I can stop a horse in Polish. 'Brrrr.'

In the evening Stan appeared to collect the horse and me (in order of importance) and return to the farm, where I ate my plate of Frau Schmidt's wretched soup and returned to the camp. The next day the farmer took me with the horse and plough to the beginning of the field, and again just left me, telling me I ought to finish it today as this field normally took two days to plough. It was a very lonely day, nothing to be seen for miles in a flat, uninteresting terrain, just me and a horse that couldn't understand plain English. At least I had something to talk to, as the beast would not keep going without a running encouragement from me of 'Hee Haw Hicks'. Somewhat surprisingly I had in fact finished by late afternoon, with my equipage somewhere in the middle of the field, when Schmidt came to check my progress and take us both in for supper — that is if his wife allowed the horse any supper (it probably fed better than I did).

When Schmidt got up to me, without a word he took the reins and started ploughing. I asked him what he was doing and he told me he was starting to plough the field. He never bothered to explain what was wrong with my ploughing; it looked all right to me.

The next day Schmidt again took the plough out with me, and this time also with Lena. My spirits rose a little. If he was going to leave me to plough a field with Lena for company the day might prove more interesting.

Alas no. We went to another field where he started ploughing up and down in what I would have regarded as the more normal manner. Lena walked to one end of the field and I started off quite happily with her, but she shook her head and pointed to Schmidt who was waving me to the other end. Schmidt ploughed a couple of furrows and condescended to explain. This was a potato field and the spuds had already been lifted, but there would still be some left in the ground so he was going over it a second time to lift whatever might be remaining. Lena was to work from one end, walking to the middle of the field picking out the spuds from the newly turned furrow, and at the centre would take her trophies back to her end of the field and gradually assemble a pile of potatoes. I was to do the same thing from the other end.

It took me just one trip up my half of a furrow to take a strong dislike to spud lifting. Thank heavens I had not been on this or any other farm a month earlier in the spud season. No wonder ex-farmworkers at *Stalag* spoke of it as hard work. Hard work? It was clearly going to be back-breaking if I was going to

Edward Lyme

do this for my half of this large field, which looked a lot bigger now that I knew what we were there for. Oh no, this called for a little column-dodging.

Schmidt was ploughing just a couple of furrows ahead of us all the time so we were both closely under his eye, with Lena working her way along the furrow from her end, filling up her basket with spuds and returning to put them on her own pile, while I was doing the same thing from the other end. The slight difference between us was that while Lena was picking up all the potatoes thrown up by the plough I was only picking up about one in four, just flicking the other three with my toe into the next furrow, where they were covered up again as Schmidt's plough passed over. The result was that while Lena's pile gradually grew into a respectable collection of *Kartoffeln*, mine remained pitifully small.

At the end of the day Schmidt looked at the piles and said there must be less left over in the field than he had thought — there would not be any point in going on for the next two days as he had intended. Did Farmer Schmidt perhaps get a first nagging doubt here about the value of *Kriegsgefangene* 8075 as a useful addition to his farm? Never mind. Further demonstrations were to follow, until all doubt was removed.

The next job I had with Lena was to complete building a haystack. Schmidt motioned her to get on the stack to distribute the hay, while I was given a hayfork to pick up the hay lying around and pass it up to her. This didn't seem too difficult, and I duly started picking up a forkful on the end of the long two-pronged hay fork and passing it up to Lena on the top.

'Pick it up,' said Schmidt.

What the hell was he talking about? I *was* picking it up. After a while he motioned Lena and me to change places, so I climbed on the stack and Lena forked up the hay. I saw what Schmidt meant. Without apparent effort Lena was picking up what looked like half a ton of hay in each forkful, a veritable mountain of a bundle about six feet in diameter. How she got it to adhere to the fork at all was a mystery to me, and the fact that she could lift it up on the end of a long-handled fork gave me considerable respect for her muscle power. After a while of this, Schmidt again motioned for a change of places, but when I tried to collect a good forkful like hers I found I couldn't lift it. I tugged and tugged, ashamed that a soldier could not lift a simple forkful of hay that a slip of a girl could throw up. Schmidt explained to me, as to a child, that the reason was that in trying to get a good forkful I was standing on one end of the bundle I was trying to lift. After some ineffectual effort to cure my incompetence he had to settle for allowing me to continue to lift the few wisps that I had started off with.

He was later well satisfied with my digging, however, but that was because he was not there to see it. One day he gave me another job with Lena, this time to dig a patch of ground immediately behind the farmhouse. This was a fairly large rectangle of earth, divided in two lengthwise by a trodden path in the middle. Lena and I had a spade apiece to dig this over, one half each. We were under the eagle eye of Frau Schmidt, who looked out of her kitchen window from time to time to make sure we were still there. Schmidt had left us to go into town.

The reader who has come this far will not need to be told how the digging proceeded. The girl on one side dug steadily at her half, the newly turned ground behind her lengthening while the unturned patch ahead grew smaller. On the other side the soldier dug slowly and with distaste, with a few poorly dug rows behind him and an unchanging and undug expanse before him, pausing every few spadefuls to stroll over to the girl to ask her the words for numbers in Polish.

The result of course was that Lena finished her half while I was still somewhere near base, and she started at the top of my half and worked backwards towards me. She didn't mind — she knew she had to work anyway while British prisoners of war could get away with it — and although we never managed to get beyond a quick kiss now and then, we were quite good pals.

Lena had just got near me, having dug the whole of her half and three-quarters of mine, when Frau Schmidt called her in to run some errand. There was only a row or two left to dig, and left on my own I completed it. I had just done so when Schmidt appeared, finding me on my own and the whole plot well dug. He congratulated me on my hard work, and said I could come in for supper now as I deserved to finish early that day after such a good job.

My day was not entirely wasted. The Schmidts are probably dead by now, and Lena perhaps a grandmother who has long forgotten digging a patch of earth with prisoner number 8075. But I can still count in Polish.

Life plays some odd tricks. This was the only time in my captivity that I worked on a farm with a girl at hand, and I had been over two years without touching a woman. I was only alone with Lena on one occasion, when quite unexpectedly Schmidt gave us both a job in the hay loft, the traditional place for a tumble. To my own surprise, and indeed astonishment in retro-spect, I didn't even make a pass at her. The moment passed and did not occur again! No doubt if I had been there a little longer nature would have taken its natural course, but it is a fact that in five years the only opportunity I had was thrown away.

Some of the chaps in *Stalag* kept a bar of soap or of chocolate in the field dressing pocket of their battledress trousers as an offering or payment if the opportunity arose. I never did this and gave Lena both soap and chocolate anyway; she said I was a good *Kavalier* even if I was the worst *Arbeiter* she had ever come across.

There was a young Scotsman in my room back in Schlüsselmühle who used to taunt the married men, especially recently married ones, with word pictures of their wives' presumed infidelities while we were all stuck in a prison camp, on the basis that 'A slice off a cut loaf is never missed.' He was probably right on the first count, but wrong on the second. Frau Schmidt missed it.

One evening when Lena, Stan and I were having our meal in the scullery, the soup was even worse than usual and the single slice of bread thinner than usual. Even Lena, who seldom complained, was moved to remark on it, and Stan who had suffered these short commons for a long time, was more vocal than usual about it.

There was a tiny passageway between the Schmidt's kitchen and our scullery, with a little table that had the loaf of bread and a knife on it. I got up, went to the passage table, and cut another slice of bread. I called through to the others 'Another slice?' Lena indicated 'No,' whether from fear of her mistress or feminine concern for the waistline I cannot say. Stan was vague, so I was satisfied with the one slice and returned to the scullery, where Star and I had half each.

We had already eaten this when Frau Schmidt tore into the room like Christ coming to cleanse the Temple.

'Someone has cut more bread; the loaf is shorter!' she screamed.

She went for Stan, not because she really thought it was him, but because he was a target without the right to answer back. I told her to calm down, I had cut the bread (much like George Washington acknowledging his misdemeanour with the cherry tree), and she was entitled to report me whenever she wished. She ranted a little more, but there was nothing she could do, and she knew it. The Poles could have been reported for wasting German food, but she knew damn well she was not giving reasonable food to her prisoner of war and could not risk tangling with the military authorities and perhaps losing cheap labour next year. It was probably the first time Frau Schmidt had lost an argument for years.

It will be clear that solely due to time of year I had so far avoided the hard work of my predecessor. But nemesis was at hand. The threshing in the village was done on a communal basis: when each farm was ready for threshing, farmhands were lent from other farms to give the threshing farmer a good work-force for the few days of threshing, and of course in his turn he would lend to the others.

I was lucky in that almost all the threshing had already been done, but there was one farm still to go, and of course the Schmidts lent me, the only real value for money they got out of me. They would have been lent a dozen good workers when they did their own threshing, but when it came to their turn to lend they kept their best two workers and palmed the other farmer off with me. If the Fair Trading Act had existed then they would probably have been charged with unfair trading.

The scene of nemesis was a very large barn with the thresher in the middle of it. The work was simple enough. The thresher was fed with corn at one end, and as it chuntered away, which it did all day, the sacks of corn filled up and the hay came out at the other end, where it was forked up on to the growing pile on one side of the barn. The forking was done by the girls, while the men tended the machine. The men were no fools.

I was put with the girls, which sounds pleasant enough, but the man who wrote the song 'Put me among the girls' clearly did not have threshing in mind.

The disposal of the hay would not have looked very hard to an observer. The girls nearest the machine forked the hay up to the lowest level of stacking, where the next girl forked it one stage higher, and so on to the top of the high barn. The trouble was that the bloody machine never stopped and the hay just kept coming and coming. I had the easiest part of the chain, right at the top where I only had to receive the forkful from the girl below and did not have to bend down to pick it up and then fork it higher up. All I had to was to distribute it evenly around the top and tread it down, but there just didn't seem to be time to do this; the stuff just kept coming as the girls themselves worked like a machine in harmony. But there was a discordant note at the top. I spread it around all right, but could not get ahead of the Amazon below me sufficiently to tread it down.

All might yet have been well if the farmer himself had not chosen to come up to the top to check my work. This particular farmer was a small and very irritable man, finding fault with even the hardest workers. When he got to the top and went stamping around to see if I had trodden it in properly, he stepped on a section which I had filled by the lightest of forkfuls, and suddenly disappeared, like Laurel and Hardy stepping into a six-feet-deep hole in an apparently shallow river.

He floundered out of it and called me the worst name he could think of. He called me a Jew. Although the Nazis' hatred of the Jews was well enough known (though the full depth of their infamy had not been revealed at that time), a prisoner of war did not normally come across it, and as I was quite amused by his disappearance in the hay, I cheerfully acknowledged that I was indeed a Jew. He knew perfectly well that I was not, but I was treading on more dangerous ground than I knew. He said he would tell Hans to keep an eye on me.

I knew all about Hans. Hans was the farmer's son, a handsome, well-built man somewhere in his mid-thirties, vaguely popping into the barn every now and then to check on the work. I had been warned about Hans, and it was clear the Polish farmhands were afraid of him. Hans was a member of the SA (*Sturm Abteilung* — storm trooper, Hitler's Brown Shirts).

I was not worried about this, and just carried on with my work. But I simply couldn't keep up the pace, and although I knew stuff would only pile up more if I stopped, I just downed my fork, climbed down, and went off to the little privy outside the barn.

The pattern next day was the same as before — that damned machine churning out more and more hay without a stop, the girls working like automatons forking the stuff up and me giving myself a break by visits to the privy. It must have been obvious to everybody else that I was dodging the column. I could not possibly have eaten enough to require 20 minutes to the lavatory every hour or so.

I was sitting on the privy seat, without even the fiction of my trousers down, when the privy door opened. It should not have opened, it was latched on the inside. It opened because Hans tore it off the latch with the force of temper, and stood there in even greater fury than Frau Schmidt with her lost slice cut off the loaf. And certainly more dangerous.

I stood up with whatever dignity I could muster, and stepped out of the privy. But Hans was in no mood for niceties.

'Get back to work!' he screamed.

I walked past him and some chance or instinct made me turn round. He had a hay fork in his hand and lunged at me as I turned. I just moved aside from it, and hit him on the jaw. He went down and for a couple of seconds lay sprawled on the ground, the two-pronged fork beside him, looking up at me. He was not hurt, and had really gone down as much from being caught off balance as anything else; I had not hit him hard, and if anything his look indicated surprise.

For my part in those two or three seconds, I was appalled. What had I done? I had not only struck a German, for which I was likely to be sent to Graudenz, but an SA man to boot. Christ, they shot you for that. (Graudenz was the punishment camp and had a similar reputation to that later applied to Belsen.)

Hans got up, picked up his fork and presented the business end to me again, but did not attempt to strike out with it. I turned and went back into the barn, Hans behind me with the fork. I climbed back up to my post and continued working. Even then I could not pretend I could keep up the solid pace of the girls, but I did not attempt to dodge the column again that day.

Nothing came of the incident. Hans would have known instinctively that I would not run around boasting of having hit an SA man, and that I would be likely to keep it to myself, as in fact I did.

It was not long after the threshing that a much more pleasant incident occurred. I was coming back from the Schmidt farm to the prison camp when I passed the door of one of the other farmhouses with the German farmer's wife standing at the door. She called to me and beckoned me in.

Inside she took me to the kitchen, bade me sit down, and placed a good meal before me. She told me she had been waiting to catch me one day to give me a meal, as she knew I worked for Frau Schmidt and the whole village knew how mean Frau Schmidt was with food. She had noticed how thin I seemed to be and felt I needed a motherly good meal to fill me up, so here it was. If there is any moral in her kindness it is one I have known all my life, that it is impossible to generalise about Germans or any other set of people by race, religion or anything else. People are people.

It was only a day or two after this unexpected supper that I left the farm. We were now into December and the guard came one night, in a blinding snowstorm, to say he had received orders that I was to be returned to *Stalag*. It was getting late and one would have expected him to leave it till the next day, especially in the abominable weather, but he was one of those people who feel that once they have an order it must be obeyed promptly. The trouble was that he could not get Schmidt to agree to turn out his horse and wagon and take me to the station, nor would any other villager do it. There was no reason why they should, it was not their responsibility. For my part I would have been quite happy to go the same night, as I had the same view of the Schmidt farm by this time as that of my Inniskilling predecessor. But if no one was going to turn out on such a night, it would just have to wait until tomorrow.

Someone did turn out. One villager got out his horse and cart and not only took me to the station, but insisted on my sitting beside him to talk to him on the journey. It was Hans.

* * *

My return to *Stalag* turned out to be for no more purpose than to take a French examination I had put in for. This was dealt with promptly, and left me stuck at *Stalag* in Fort 13.

I was very glad to meet my old pal George Sketchley who had by this time got himself a *Stalag* office job in the administration block, which put him in the realm of being 'in the rackets'. It also gave him that indefinable change of mental attitude which enabled him to settle down comfortably in the awful Fort 13 as 'home'. I was again struck with the contrast between the attitudes of the *Stalag* workers, who were well settled in and not only liked the place but strongly resisted any encroachment on their 'corners', and the transient types like myself who were only too glad to be out of it.

The Fort had not changed. There were still the three-tiered shelves for communal sleeping, and these wooden mess bunks had got even dirtier with the years. I found myself a top place as was my wont, but I might have been better off somewhere else. At this time *Stalag* was undergoing an invasion of bugs, and the bunks were infested with them. One morning I woke up and found I could not open my left eye. George looked at it and told me why. I had a bug bite which had so swollen the whole eye that the eyelid would not move.

This would not normally have warranted a hospital bed, but when I went to the Revier for treatment it so happened that they had a spare bed, so I spent a week or so in the fort hospital. They were of course quite used to patients with this sort of thing in Fort 13, and when my eye filled up with pus, simply squeezed it out. This was only a minor passing incident in my *Stalag* life, but one remembered well enough as an amusement I could happily have done without.

All in all Fort 13 was not a desirable residence in my eyes, and I wished for a transport. Despite my proven incompetence as a road builder, construction worker and farmer, there was always a certain adventure in an unknown transport, and a little of Fort

13 went a long way with me. Christmas was now close, and once that was over who knew what the New Year might bring.

When one is in a frying pan, it is a mistake to wish oneself out of it. It might be more uncomfortable outside.

Almost on top of Christmas — in fact on 22 December, 1942, when we were right out of Red Cross and a delivery of parcels was expected in a day or two — I was summoned to join an *Arbeitskommando* to leave *Stalag* the following morning for a place called Wahlstatt, which was apparently about 15 kilometres west of Bromberg (Bydgoswcz).

When we assembled next morning for transport to Wahlstatt, foodless, I wished for once that I was staying behind at *Stalag*, at least until Christmas was over. I could hardly have foreseen that I would be back in *Stalag* within a week, but not in Fort 13. I would be escorted to Fort 16, to the cells of the punishment block — and not sorry to find myself there in one piece, having been in the meantime starved, nearly shot, walled up in a chimney, almost frozen to death, and locked up in a police cell in handcuffs.

In short, I was in for a merry Christmas.

6

Merry Christmas

There were 39 of us, with half-a-dozen guards, the whole party being in the charge of a nasty-tempered little *Unteroffizier*. We were going to take over a farm where Russian prisoners had been working, and none of us was very keen on the idea. To start with it was almost Christmas 1942, and we had left *Stalag* just before the Christmas Red Cross parcels arrived — which meant that even if we got good food we would have nothing English for Christmas. Then the reports of the camp were bad, which put us in a pessimistic mood. On top of this none of us knew each other, as it was a scratch working party got together at the last moment from the remnants of other working parties who happened to be in *Stalag* the previous day. All of this, together with the fact that the *Unteroffizier* had already hit one or two men with the butt of his pistol, made it look as though it would be a not-quite-so-merry-Christmas.

We entrained at Thorn in the usual cattle truck, and after a journey that took us to about mid-afternoon were roused at what appeared to be a set of sidings near a station. I never knew the name of the station, but it was evidently a junction from which we would get to Wahlstatt by local small-gauge line.

The cattle truck we had come in thus far was at least full-size: we now had to pile in to a half-size truck on a narrow-gauge line rather similar to the type one sees at holiday camps for children's rides. It was bitterly cold, we had not had anything to eat or drink since morning, and we sat tightly packed in the truck waiting for it to start. We were there a couple of hours, all sitting in silence, each wrapped up in his own private misery, and by this time in darkness.

It was during this wretched period that one of the guards came to the door of the truck and said that it would still be an hour before we could start, and in the meantime he would leave the door open so that we could have fresh air. This was received in silence, except for my own sarcastic comment from my corner: 'That's very magnanimous of him.'

There was a moment's silence. Then a voice from the darkness of the opposite corner said bitterly,

'That's all we needed; we've got an educated bastard with us.'

Eventually we started off and arrived at the little station of Wahlstatt at around eight o'clock. The village was a couple of miles away from the station, and a boy was waiting with a large farm wagon to take us to it. We all got aboard and drove over a horrible rutted road to Wahlstatt. It was not a prepossessing looking place, even allowing for the fact that we saw it first in the dark. There were only a few dim lights and obviously no electricity. This proved to be an old school building which was at least clean inside, but for light there was only one oil lamp and the depressing effect of this low flickering light is difficult to describe.

We had not eaten all day and the farmer who was to employ us sent some soup for us, but despite our hunger we could only eat a little of it as it had been made with rotten potatoes and smelt awful.

The following day, Christmas Eve, we learned we were not to start work until the 27th, so we had the opportunity of taking stock of our surroundings and getting to know one another. This is a simple job in a prison camp, and we were soon all acquainted and standing about in groups or in twos and threes talking or playing cards. Some attempted to walk round the compound for exercise, but as the compound was closely wired round the school, the few steps to and fro were even more like being in a cage than usual.

I found a friend in Harry Rodham, a young man of about my own age who came from Newcastle — one of the few Geordies whose speech I could understand. He had, like myself, just left a good friend with whom he had been since captivity started nearly three years before, and we had much in common. (His friend's name was Les Alsop, whom I met myself in a later camp, and with whom I subsequently made a successful escape in spring 1945.)

The midday soup was again inedible, and we began to discuss plans to escape. Several were considering it, but I believe Harry and I were the only ones for going immediately, while discipline among the guards was still a bit relaxed over Christmas. If we did, others would have to go pretty much at the same time, as security would certainly be tightened up after an escape. We had of course no time for detailed preparation, but I had seen my friend Jim O'Donnell make four carefully planned escapes only to be caught on some trivial piece of bad luck, and the experiences of others had shown that an unplanned escape stood a reasonable chance with a proportionate amount of good luck. This may not seem logical, but as many escapes got through by luck as by planning. We got no further than this on the Christmas Eve, and the matter was left until the following day.

Next day produced a cut in the bread ration (on Christmas Day!) and an even worse soup than before, and Harry and I decided it was now or not at all. Our preparations were simple enough, and consisted of putting on two of everything (it was still below zero outside) and packing up our kit in the vague hope that we might eventually see it again if recaptured.

We were very lucky for food, as although I had nothing Harry had recently had a Canadian Red Cross parcel which was still intact. A Canadian parcel contained biscuits, milk, Spam and corned beef, just right for a 'walk'. Our plan was perforce simple enough. We would walk to Bromberg, jump on a goods train for Danzig, and hope to stow away in a Swedish vessel.

It was fairly dark by five o'clock, and quietly and without any leave-taking Harry and I slipped out of the billet and round to the back of the building. No guard was in sight: we had little trouble getting through the barbed wire and hurried away across the fields.

Although we were the first couple away, we knew that at least four more couples were also escaping that night (as a matter of fact another 11 men besides ourselves made the attempt: all were recaptured within 12 hours), and it was obvious that our departure would not remain undiscovered long. It therefore behoved us to put as many miles as possible between ourselves and the camp before pursuit started. The chance of getting right away to Sweden and thence to England was very small, but if we were recaptured we didn't want to be taken by the *Unteroffizier* or his minions, as we felt certain we would get a 'doing over' in that event. (As it happened the last three men to get away were recaptured before they had gone half a mile and the *Unteroffizier* did no more than put them in the cellar for the night without food, which was considerably milder treatment than Harry and I received at the hands of our captor later.)

We had been going across fields for a couple of hours when we realized we had completely lost our sense of direction. We decided, after some thought, that the best thing we could do would be to get on to the road and walk along the ditch. If we heard anyone approaching or saw any bicycle lamp or car headlights we could lie flat in the ditch till the danger had passed. In this way we would be able to get along much more quickly with less fatigue and, most important of all, we would be able to see the signposts and avoid walking in a circle, which we suspected we had been so far.

We got to what appeared to be a main road and followed it. We had no idea which way to go, but shortly after we got on to it we heard a pistol shot about a mile away and, assuming that it came from the now-alarmed guards at the camp we had escaped from, went in the opposite direction. We kept well to the side of the road, I in front and Harry behind. Several times we had to get down into the ditch to allow a car or cycle to pass, and on more than one occasion my deafness (my sense of hearing had been deteriorating ever since Calais) would have caused us to be caught had it not been for Harry's quick action. He would hear a car approaching and, calling out to me to get down, would lie down in the ditch. I however, not having heard either car or Harry, would go blithely on until Harry scrambled out of the ditch again, flung me down and dived down after me, sometimes when the car was almost on top of us.

We carried on in this manner for some hours. Each time we came to a village or even a single house on the road we made a wide detour across the fields, keeping the road in sight all the time. This was not difficult on such occasions as Polish roads — and German ones for that matter — are lined with regularly spaced trees, and the course of the main road can be discerned from a considerable distance away, even at night. We were getting pretty tired by this time, and we still had not found a signpost to indicate whether we were on the right road for Bromberg or not. Signposts we had passed in plenty, but they had been for small villages, none of which we knew. At last, at what we judged to be about midnight, we came to a crossroads, at which was a signpost with the magic name 'Bromberg' thereon. But alas, the arm on which it was painted pointed along the road we had just travelled. We had been walking for the past six hours in the opposite direction to the one we wanted to take.

There was, we finally considered, little damage done. We could continue along the road we were now on and get to Zempelburg, a smaller town than Bromberg, but one where we could get a train to Konitz and there with luck another train for Danzig. We decided to go on another ten miles or so that same night, and sought a safe spot where we could rest a little while before continuing. We found a hollow on top of a small hill which sloped down towards the crossroads, and there we lay for about half an hour. So far despite the cold our long walk, combined with all the clothing we had on, had kept us quite warm. However, it was now getting much colder, and although we had not noticed this, we became aware of it as soon as we tried to drink some milk. We were terribly thirsty and we opened the tin of Nestles milk in Harry's pack, but it was frozen and would not pour, so we took the lid right off and tried to eat it with a spoon. It was so cold, however, that despite our thirst we could not stomach more than half a spoonful each. We ate a biscuit and then resumed our journey.

It had been a great hindrance to our progress to have to skirt every village we came to, for there was one every two or three kilometres along the road, and we decided that from now on we would go straight through them, the extra speed gained thereby outweighing the extra risk. This we did, and in this manner passed through several villages without meeting a soul. We were by now feeling extremely tired as well as thirsty, and had been on the lookout for some time for a single farm; if we could find one there was just a chance that it might belong to a Pole, and if not, a single farmer on his own away from a village was not likely to attempt to arrest us. We continued for many kilometres without sighting a likely place, and at last we decided to tackle one of a group of three standing in the middle of some fields.

Long before we reached the farmhouse the dogs of the farms had announced our coming by excited barking, but it didn't seem to wake anyone for no lights appeared and the house we were making for remained silent. We debated the idea of going straight into the barn and continuing as soon as we were rested, but our thirst was acute and we finally knocked on the door.

When it was opened there stood before us an elderly man clad in a long white nightshirt and a peaked cap with the red, white and black button of Government service on it. The man was evidently a postman or porter or something similar, and presumably thought to impress his nocturnal visitors with his importance, hence the headgear.

He asked us what we wanted, and as I could think of no reasonable excuse for being abroad at that hour (it was about three o'clock) told him we were Englishmen and we wanted something to drink and somewhere to sleep for the night. He was plainly frightened, and called over his shoulder to someone in the house to fetch some water. He never moved from the doorway and was obviously standing guard in case we should try to enter the house. The water was brought and we drank some; we drank very little as a matter of fact because it was so cold — with the temperature outside below zero we were too cold to drink much. The old man said he had no room in the house for us and begged us not to stay in his barn; if we stayed in the barn, he said, he would be duty-bound to report us and he wanted to get back to bed; if we went away he promised to say nothing. We had little choice, for although he obviously had no desire to go a mile to the village after the *Burgermeister* at this time in the morning, had we stayed in the barn he would have been too afraid of authority to ignore our presence and would have undoubtedly reported us. So we left him and went on.

We finally realised we would find no barn in the open, so we decided to chance getting into one in a village. The trouble with this was that although there was little danger of waking anyone while we were getting into a farmyard, the village dogs would probably raise a chorus and alarm someone. Still it had to be chanced, and as luck would have it the next village we came to had a barn on the outskirts attached to the first house. We found the big doors bolted on the inside, but managed to force one of them sufficiently to admit our bodies.

It was pitch black inside the barn and we had to strike one of our few matches to see where we were. (There is more in this than meets the eye. If we were recaptured we were so far only charge-able with the offence of escaping, an internationally recognised crime, and one that is punishable under the Geneva Convention by not more than 28 days' solitary confinement. The action of bringing an open light, such as a match or cigarette, into a barn, however, was a serious crime in Germany and punishable by two years' hard labour. Anyone who, by such an action, set fire to a barn would be liable to the death penalty.) On one side of the barn the straw was piled up to a height of about ten feet, and on to this we climbed. We were going to stay here all Boxing Day, so we made ourselves comfortable deep down in the straw, with our two overcoats on top of us as blankets. Despite this however and the fact that we were huddled against each other, it was impossible to sleep for the cold, and we lay there shivering for the rest of that night and the whole of Boxing Day.

On Boxing Day morning we heard the farmer come into the barn to cut some chaff for the horses. A girl, whom we presumed to be his daughter, climbed on to our stack to throw some sheaves down to her father, but we lay still and astonishingly she did not see us. During the day we managed to eat the tin of milk by sucking it slowly off a spoon, and we opened the tin of Spam from Harry's invaluable parcel. Although we reckoned we had walked some 30 kilometres the previous night without eating, it was only with difficulty that we ate our Spam and bread, since both were frozen. We were glad when twilight came and we could get away again.

As soon as it was dark (at about four o'clock) we got out of the barn by the same way that we had got in and, after skirting the village which was still full of moving figures, got on to the road again. We were a little too anxious to get back on the road again, and we regained it only two or three hundred yards outside the village. As a consequence we passed half a dozen people in the next half mile or so, but fortunately none of them stopped us. To those that showed any interest at all I called out 'Gross Weinachten! Heil Hitler!' and, receiving a similar reply, we passed on. One man on a bicycle looked at us keenly as he rode past and must have recognised our uniforms for he stopped his bike and got off, starting after us. After a moment he evidently decided to do nothing about it, for he mounted his bike again and rode on in the direction of the village.

We continued along the road for the next five or six hours, not stopping to skirt villages but going straight through. We passed a few people in the early part of the evening but as the hour grew later they disappeared into their houses and we were once more passing through silent villages.

At about ten o'clock we approached the village of Sassenau. It marked an important stage in our journey, for it was the first village inside the *Kreis* (district) of Zempelburg, and once past it we would be outside Kreis Bromberg, in which we had been since our escape, and therefore unlikely to be taken back to Wahlstatt in the event of recapture.

On the outskirts of the village was a board marked 'Sassenau — Kreis Zempelburg' and we stopped for a moment to congratulate ourselves (a trifle prematurely perhaps) and to consider our position. The query before us was whether we should go straight through the village as we had been doing or whether we should take to the fields until we were past it. The wisest course was obviously to avoid it, since Sassenau was a bigger village than the others we had passed through, and we were now only about 12 miles from Zempelburg, where we hoped to jump a train. On the other hand the detour would be a much longer and more tiring business, whereas we could be through the village within ten minutes if we kept on the road — providing of course that our luck held.

We finally decided to stay on the road, and accordingly carried on. We had not gone far when we heard footsteps coming towards us, and not wishing to take unnecessary chances, we hid in an alleyway between two houses. I remember flattening my back and hands against the wall and thinking with some surprise, 'This is how they do it in the films.' The footsteps passed, but meanwhile we had become interested in the games of three children whom we could see through the badly blacked-out window of the house against whose wall we were standing. We wondered whether they were Poles or Germans, and it looked so warm and inviting inside the house that we half-decided to knock and find out, but fortunately their mother came into the room and spoke to them loudly in German, so we changed our minds.

We continued along the road, through the village, past the Police Station, and out of the village the other side. We were just passing the last few houses when a man passed us on the road. He had gone a few steps past us when we heard him stop, and a moment later he called out to us to stop also. We ignored him and carried on, but he shouted out and looking back we saw he had drawn a revolver, so we had no recourse but to obey him. He came towards us, still holding the revolver, and I went to meet him. I saw he was a soldier, but as it was so dark he came very close to me to peer into my face, and I saw he had the silver braid on his collar of a sergeant of the *Wehrmacht*.

'Where are you going?' he demanded.

'To Zempelburg,' I said (which was true).

'What for?' was his next question.

'Oh, we're catching a train there" I replied (which was also true. I hoped).

'Who are you?' he asked. Then, before I could think of a reply to this one, he looked down at my uniform and said, 'You're not Germans. Come on, who are you?'

He looked at Harry who just shrugged his shoulders. He still had the revolver in his hand, and we were obviously caught, so the easiest thing to do was to get it over and done with and hope for better luck next time.

'We're escaped English prisoners,' I told him.

'Oh, are you,' he said. 'Right. About turn, quick march. And don't talk!'

So perforce, we about-turned and quick-marched.

We were a little puzzled by this. As I have already explained, escaping from a prisoner-of-war camp is not a very serious crime, and we had expected to be taken back into Sassenau to be locked up in the local Police Station till the morning and then sent back to *Stalag* for a week or two's 'solitary', which would be the end of the matter. This sergeant, however, was marching us away from the village, and we were a little apprehensive, since the Geneva Convention was probably a closed book to him and he might be intending to shoot us for all we knew.

We had only gone a couple of dozen yards when he stopped at a house and knocked on the door. When it was opened, by a soldier, the sergeant gave some instructions and marched us on. I tried to stop and talk with him but he would have none of it, shouting and brandishing his revolver.

We went to what appeared to be a farm, through a gate and into a square formed by the farm buildings, with a tall chimney stack, apparently unconnected with anything, in the middle of the square.

He motioned us to stand up against one of the walls and then announced his intention of shooting us as spies. I brought out my *Stalag* disc and showed it to him, demanding to be sent back to *Stalag* for trial in accordance with the Geneva Convention. He took no notice at all, except to say that he was not interested in all this, and as far as he was concerned, we were spies. This was ridiculous as we were in uniform and had admitted our nationality and I told him so, but he paid no attention.

At this point, a lance-corporal appeared and the sergeant said he was only joking with us, and would only send the lance-corporal for a key to lock us up. We often wondered later whether it really was a joke or not, as the lance-corporal's appearance seemed to be quite fortuitous.

When the key was brought, he searched us thoroughly, taking everything except our handkerchiefs. We wondered where we were to be locked up for the night, but even we were surprised when he took the key, opened the fire-door of the chimney stack in the centre of the yard and motioned us to get in.

The iron door was slammed to and locked with a huge padlock and we were left inside the chimney. It was of course pitch dark inside, but a light would have been superfluous. Standing against one side of the chimney we could touch the opposite wall without raising our arms for more than a fraction, and although Harry, who was much shorter than I, could at least lay down after a fashion, I could not. We computed the length and breadth of our prison to be about four feet by three feet; it was difficult to estimate its height, but we thought something over 50 feet, and as it was blocked up near the top we could not see the sky.

We had been in there about an hour when the door was opened and we saw two vague figures outside. One of them spoke to the other and we recognised the voice of the sergeant. His companion did not speak, but thrust two blankets and a piece of bread into the chimney. Then the door was shut again.

The blankets showed at least a little humane thought on someone's part, but they were not a lot of good as they were of poor material and very thin. The bread was very useful, and when we picked it up from the corner where it had been thrust we found what appeared to be two pieces. A moment later we discovered that only the top piece was bread, the other being a cardboard box which proved to contain some *Junaks* (a cheap Polish cigarette, sold by the Germans only to prisoners of war) and a box of matches. These were more valuable to us at that time than either the blankets or the bread, but we had to be very careful in smoking in case a glow showed through any cracks there may be in the fire-door, for discovery might have caused trouble for our unknown benefactor. We wondered whether he was a Pole who had brought the cigarettes from a prisoner of war, but this did not sound feasible since Poles were not allowed abroad at this time of night. Again he must obviously have had some connection with the sergeant, since he was responsible for the blankets and bread. We finally gave it up and lay down to sleep.

We were both dog-tired but although we lay huddled together (perforce, since I could not lay down without bending my body, and Harry had to bend his to fit in with mine; even like this we were touching all four walls of the chimney), we could not sleep for the cold, which was now intense.

We finally sat up and talked for the rest of the night. Something about the situation must have sharpened our sense of humour, or maybe we were merely overstrung, but I remember Harry making a remark about it being 'lucky we didn't suffer from claustrophobia' and we laughed over it for hours.

Morning came and with it a little light. There were no appreciable cracks in the fire-door to let in light as we had hoped, but there was a small hole about a quarter of an inch in diameter in the door and this admitted sufficient light to enable us to see each other, and to guess roughly what the time was. We also became quite accurate in pissing through this hole.

No one came to us during the day, and when darkness fell we

realised we were going to spend another night in the chimney. We were feeling the cold badly by this time, since, apart from the temperature and the lack of anything warm to drink, we were unable to move about and keep ourselves warm by any form of exercise. During our talk in the course of the morning Harry had told me of a minor accident which had befallen his sister some time before the war — an account of which had included a description of his sister tucked up in bed with a glass of hot milk beside her — and for the rest of that day and most of the following day I was unable to rid my mind of a picture of being tucked up in a bed with a glass of hot milk, for which at that time I would gladly have given my gratuity.

We had already settled down for the night when we heard the key in the lock. When the door was opened and the sergeant's voice told us to get out we were so cold it was difficult to get through the opening, which was only about 18 inches square.

Outside we learned that we were to stay in the chimney, but he had brought us a drink. There was a man standing with him holding a steaming jug and a couple of mugs, and he now came forward. Imagine our surprise when the man proved to be a British sergeant and the drink English tea!

The sergeant forbade anyone to speak except in German, but the English sergeant managed to tell us that he came from a nearby prison camp of 40 men. They had been told of the 'Prisoners in the Tower' as they called us (before the war, a British officer named Baillie-Stewart was accused of treason and imprisoned in the Tower of London, where the press labelled him: 'The Prisoner in the Tower'), and had asked to be allowed to make us a drink from the tea in their Red Cross parcels. The comradely act was the more praiseworthy as they had received no parcels for two weeks and had only just enough tea between them to make us a brew. The sergeant refused our request to be allowed to run up and down a bit to exercise our limbs, but promised to allow us out for a few minutes the next day during daylight.

We drank our tea, as welcome a drink as may be imagined, and prepared to get back into the chimney. The English sergeant asked us if we would like some straw, and we were allowed to wait outside while he fetched some. We thanked our benefactor again and climbed back in.

I remember that before the war there was a popular advertisement for tea which said 'Tea revives you!' Never was an advertisement more true. Ten minutes before we had been lying down on the damp floor of the chimney shivering and miserable, but now, warmed by the tea and with fresh straw to lie on, we felt not only cheerful but actually quite comfortable, and we pulled the straw round us and slept quite well that night.

We awoke, shivering, just before dawn, but nobody came to the chimney until noon. Then the door was opened and the sergeant told us to get out and to go into the nearest barn, where we found two plates of boiled potatoes. We ate as much as we could, and then under the eye of the sergeant ran up and down the yard for ten minutes or so, after which we were again locked up in the chimney.

No one came again during daylight, and we began to wonder how long we were to be left there. However, a few hours after darkness had fallen (it was about eight o'clock we subsequently discovered) the light of a torch showed through the hole in the door and we heard the key in the lock. When the door was opened we saw two men, one a sergeant, the other a *Wehrmacht* lance corporal, who was holding the torch. This man told us in quite good English that he had come to take us back to *Stalag*, and we were to get ready now.

We must have presented a curious sight to him. We were sitting huddled up together with the blankets over our heads and draped round our shoulders like Red Indian squaws, and when we tried to get out we found we couldn't move. It was so cold that we were already doubting our own survival if we spent another night there. Eventually we got out and had the satisfaction of seeing the fire door of that wretched chimney locked behind us.

The *Gefreiter* (lance-corporal) seemed quite a decent fellow, and we were very glad to see some sign of *Stalag* authority at last. He took us to the little English working camp, and asked us whether we would like to spend the night with our comrades, as he didn't think it practicable to start for *Stalag* that night. We were of course only too glad, and he and the sergeant went off leaving Harry and I inside the prison camp. The sergeant took the precaution of taking our boots, overcoats and trousers from us, which was a typical piece of German stupidity, for if we wanted to escape again we now had 40 friends who would be only too pleased to give us their clothing if we wanted it. These men were extremely good to us, providing us with a meal containing a Red Cross stew (probably the only one in the camp) and raking some more tea up from somewhere.

At about ten o'clock the *Gefrieter* from *Stalag* came in and spoke to us. He said it wasn't possible to get to *Stalag* that night, but he was not at all keen to stay in this village, as he would have to stay with the sergeant. He thought the sergeant an objectionable person, who by reason of his superior rank could order the *Gefreiter* about, and was apparently already doing so in a manner that the *Gefreiter* thought quite unpleasant. He suggested therefore that we take the midnight train to a small town at the end of the line, a town whose name I have forgotten but which was only half-an-hour's travelling distance away. There we would put up at the local *Gasthaus* for the night and travel on to Bromberg and thence to Thorn in the morning.

It sounded a reasonable idea, and we were not at all averse to sleeping in a *Gasthaus*; it would be a new experience. It was, but not quite as we had anticipated.

We retrieved our boots, trousers and overcoats from the sergeant, as well as our cigarettes and personal belongings which he had taken on Boxing night. Then, at about half-past eleven, having thanked our friends in the camp, we left and caught the midnight train.

In the train we got to know our new guard a little better. He proved to be quite friendly, and told us his name was Henry and that he was a censor at *Stalag*. Despite the fact that he was hunch-backed and with a far from handsome-looking face he fancied himself as a ladies' man, and during the whole of the following day as we were travelling he tried to date various girls whom we met in railway carriages, in all cases without success.

We finally got to the end of the line, and got out. The few other passengers on the train walked quickly off the platform, but we stood there a little uncertain of where to go. The station master came up, a grizzled old man carrying a lantern. Then the following Rob Wilton-ish conversation took place:

Henry: 'I've got two English prisoners here, and we want to put up at the *Gasthaus* for the night.'

Station master: 'Oh, there ain't no *Gasthaus* 'ere.'

'Well then, they'll have to sleep in the police cells.'

'Oh, there ain't no police station 'ere.'

'What? No police station? Where's the nearest?'

'Three kilos down the road. Place called Monkhausen.'

'Can't go that far at this time of night. Isn't there a hotel?'

'Oh, there ain't no hotel or *Gasthaus* or anything like that 'ere.'

'Well, we'll have to sleep in the station room.'

'Oh, you can't do that. Against regulations.'

'Well, we'll have to knock up a private house. I suppose we can do that?'

'Oh, no. No one round here's got any room.'

Henry would not give in and spent the best part of an hour trying to arrange for us to stay at the station, but to no purpose, and it was finally decided that we should go on to Monkhausen and stay at the police station.

We walked the three kilometres to Monkhausen and found the place dark and silent, as one would expect of a village at two o'clock in the morning. Harry and I were not anxious to find the police station ourselves for it meant we would spend the night in the cells, but anything was better than walking about at this time of morning with the temperature well below freezing, and since the police station was not immediately in sight, we walked through the village shouting at the top of our voices, *'Polizei! Polizei!'* It was rather a peculiar situation for escapees, to be putting ourselves to the trouble of shouting out for the police, so anxious were we to find them, but we wasted our breath. Had we been on the run no doubt one would have been standing at each end of the village, but since we were trying to find them our cries were in vain. Not a light showed anywhere, no one questioned us, no policeman appeared. (Murmurs of 'Never there when you want them!')

We walked right through the village in this manner and not a soul appeared. Harry and I were feeling pleased, for we thought it now certain that Henry would knock at a private house and we should spend a good night and get a breakfast in the morning. But Henry was persistent and at last discovered the police station, which was almost the last building in the village.

We knocked at the door. We banged on the door panels. We went round and tapped on every window, and finally went back to the door and kicked it heartily. But no policeman showed his head.

From the official notice board outside the house next door we presumed this to be the policeman's sleeping quarters. We found the door unlocked and went in, calling out *'Polizei!'* again and clattering up and down the little stone corridor in our iron-studded loots. But still no policeman appeared.

As a last resort we opened the doors in the passage and found one of them to be the door of a bedroom. In bed was a policeman, fast asleep, with his uniform lying over the back of the chair, and on the chair beside him his helmet and a revolver. I went over and shook him. He opened his eyes, looked at us, grabbed his helmet and put it on, then took his revolver and pointed it at us, sitting up in bed. (I know it sounds incredible but it happens to be true.)

Finally, when Henry had explained matters, he got up and dressed, and then took us round to the police station. He ordered us to turn our pockets out, but we held on to our cigarettes and one box of matches and he did not search us very strictly. Then he produced a pair of handcuffs and handcuffed my left wrist to Harry's right, after which we were marched downstairs to the cells.

The cell — which was guarded by double doors with double bolts which would have done credit to a bank's strong room — was a very small one, but quite warm as it was heated by a tiled stove in one corner. The actual fire was outside, and was tended by the policemen themselves. Since the tiles were still warm the fire had been well stocked up before the police had all gone to bed.

The doors were closed and the bolts shot home, and we heard the policeman's boots retreating up the stairs. Then we started manipulating our wrists to see if we could get the handcuffs off, and within five minutes we had done so. My previous description of 'a pair of handcuffs' is perhaps not quite correct. German handcuffs at that time consisted of a length of chain with a lock at one end. The chain was put round the wrist and one link fastened, then the other end fastened in a like manner to the other wrist and the lock shut on the appropriate link. In this way it is possible to get the handcuff the exact size of the wrist. But if they have been fastened inaccurately, as these had been, it is not a difficult matter to get them off.

The wooden bed was too small for both of us so we just sat side by side talking. Finally we began to doze off, but before we could fall asleep we heard our gaoler coming down the stairs again. As he undid the bolts of the first door we struggled to get the handcuffs on again, but they wouldn't go. The policeman undid the bolts of the second door and still we hadn't got them on, so as he opened the door I put them in my battle dress pocket and we sat there with our hands together. He said he had just come down to tell us that he was going to wake us up at six o'clock and if was now four. Then he went, without noticing that we had no handcuffs on.

Before we were 'wakened' at six o'clock we managed to get the handcuffs on again, and punctually at six we were taken out of the cell and the handcuffs were officially removed. We expected to get something to eat, but although the office now seemed to be alive with police, no one seemed to think we were worth feeding. When we asked for something we were told we would get it later. We never did, either then or throughout the day during the return to *Stalag*.

Henry arrived at eight o'clock and we caught the train for Bromberg, where an *Unteroffizier* from *Stalag* and a private met us and took us on to Thorn, which we reached in the late evening. We went straight to Fort 14, the 'Bunker'[1], and into the cells.

We were tried the next day and our sentences came through on New Year's Eve. They were surprisingly light. I got seven days and Harry, who had a previous 'conviction' got fourteen. We went into the punishment cells late on New Year's Eve, thus making an admirable start to 1943.

---

1 Long-term prisoners of war in Stalag XXA, all captured in 1940, seem to have used a different form of speech to subsequent prisoners, if films and television series are anything to go by. We always called the cells The Bunker, whereas I have noticed it seems to have been called The Cooler in other camps. Similarly, other prisoners in German hands apparently called themselves Kriegies, using the first half of the German word Kriegsgefangene meaning war prisoner, whereas if we used the German word at all we called ourselves by the second half, slightly anglicised to Gefangeners; this was at least a little more accurate, as it would mean prisoners: Kriegies would mean 'war-ies'. Most noticeable to me has been the use elsewhere of the word Goon for the guards. I never heard this word as a synonym for guards until after the war; we either called them by the English word guards, or the German word Posten; or more commonly of course simply Bastards.

7

A Room with a View

A spell in the cells of the Bunker was no hardship at all. We were supposed to subsist on bread and water, but successive occupants had established a system of bribes with the guards and we had our Red Cross parcels, so there was both food and cigarettes available, with an hour's exercise in the yard each day when Harry and I could stroll round in pleasant conversation.

I also met an old friend in the Bunker, Sergeant Jim O'Donnell of the Irish Guards. This brave man had made so many escape attempts — always on his own — that after his last effort they had made him cook in the Bunker, thus effectively stopping further efforts. It was perhaps just as well. He was glad to see me again and confided in me part of his experience in his last escape; he was clearly too cautious to tell even me too much, but it seemed he had this time fallen into the hands of the Gestapo. They had told him they knew all about Fort 14 and the easy time prisoners had in the cells, and he need not think he was going to be released for a holiday in Fort 14 until he told them all about his presumed civilian helpers. In fact there weren't any, Jim always worked on his own, but whatever they did to him he now had a limp — and still had it when I met him after the war. When they were satisfied he knew nothing of interest to them, they let *Stalag* know they had got him and he was released into *Stalag* hands.

When my time was up I returned to Fort 13, where I again met George Sketchley. As he was now on the headquarters staff he knew all about my escape with Harry, and told me that as the others who had escaped that night were all caught fairly quickly and — nothing heard of Harry and me for some days — the word went round that we had both been shot. I was glad to be able to assure him that, like Mark Twain's death, the report was exaggerated.

In due course Harry joined me and we mucked in together for a short time, but not for long as in that spring of 1943 I was suddenly sent on a transport, so suddenly that I was only able to shout the news to Harry when the truck taking me to the station passed a group of workers which included Harry.

This time I was one of a half-dozen replacements going to an existing camp. We entrained at Thorn, travelled on the Berlin line to a junction called Nakel, and then on the Konitz line to Zempelburg (Polish Sepolno).

Escapers were never sent to farms again, but to camps that were guarded in the more normal way. In this sense Zempelburg was fairly small — having 90 prisoners and 10 guards with a Jerry sergeant as *Kommandant* — but it was a regular camp with standard barbed-wire fence and under constant guard.

The camp was on the top of a hill about a mile outside the town of Zempelburg, and next to a sawmill, where we were to work. The firm was Ingbau Hellmann, and was engaged in the production of prefabricated wooden buildings of various kinds. At that time the practice was to march the prisoners out to the mills in the morning where the *Betriebsmeister* (works manager) would allocate groups of individuals to various jobs. There was one occasion when one bright lad avoided getting any job at all by hiding behind a pile of planks when the jobs were given out, and then hanging on to a single plank of wood throughout the day, so that whenever a *Meister* or guard was about he would put the plank on his shoulder and walk about purposefully. He later said he would never do it again, as it was hard work.

There were of course stacks of planks all over the place, but no one ever called them anything else but the German word *Bretter*. The *Bretter* were quite useful for a little privacy now and again.

I did not work in the sawmills very long, as shortly after I got to Zempelburg the *Kommandant* decided it was time the camp had an official interpreter and I got the job. I cannot remember any of the jobs I did while I was working on the site, but as no one in the camp suffered any amputations it is clear that I never got near the handsaws.

There was one person on the site who had suffered the loss of a thumb at some time in the past. This was a lady of such bulk and weight she was known as Two-ton. She was so tough that according to legend she had cut her thumb off one day when working with the circular saw, and simply threw it over her shoulder and carried on working. The story was no doubt apocryphal, but the fact that it was told at all was a tribute of admiration to her toughness. She had a friend, named The Princess, a lady of slatternly habit and unsurpassing ugliness. It was commonly said in the camp that these two ladies were doxy to about half the camp.

I never met anyone in Zempelburg who acknowledged coupling with either of them. I dare say there were one or two brave souls who took the opportunity of a quick rogering behind the *Bretter*, but half the camp, no. A bout with Two-ton would have been a bold enterprise not be lightly entered into, and the very thought of congress with the Princess would, for most men, cause the most throbbing ardour to wilt like a suddenly dead flower. It was nevertheless constantly claimed that they both had lovers in the camp.

I met a number of old friends in this camp. Denis was already there; the senior British NCO was Sergeant Jack Blower who was an old friend from Rittel; and Les Alsop. I had worked with Les on working parties out of *Stalag* prior to the German invasion of Russia and my own move to Schlusselmuhle, and we had become good friends. But I had not known his second name, and when I met him at Zempelburg was both surprised and pleased to find this was the Les Alsop my escape companion Harry Rodham had talked about so much. At that time we could not foresee that in the then distant future we were to share an eventual and finally successful escape.

I also met two prisoners who were new to me then but long-standing friends themselves, Phin Phillips and Doug Brunger, and had not long been at Zempelburg before Doug and I planned an escape. This was not to be a hasty affair like the last one but a carefully planned venture — not routed the 'short' way to the Baltic coast in the very outside hope of stowing away on a ship to Sweden, but involving a trek of well over 1,000 miles through Germany, the whole of France to the Pyrenees, through Spain and into Gibraltar. Whether we would have made it, or even got far, is only academic now, but we were serious enough, and I even wangled a trip to *Stalag* to see the forgers about the preparation of identity cards for us. When the *Kommandant* in Zempelburg sought an interpreter, Jack Blower recommended me for the job with part intention that it might prove useful to Doug and myself in our escape plans. The whole scheme fell to the ground when Doug was unexpectedly returned to *Stalag*, and I mucked in with Phin for the rest of my time at Zempelburg, which in fact proved to be for the rest of the war.

Phin was a Jew, and, protected by his British uniform, was among the minority of Jews who spent the war years in Nazi Germany and survived. We shared one of the three up-and-down bunks in the Staff room, which was Room No.1 out of seven prisoners' rooms in the camp and occupied by the three official prisoner staff, the senior NCO Jack Blower, the medical orderly, the interpreter and our own three muckers.

Not very long after my appointment as *Dolmetscher* Jack Blower was returned to *Stalag* and his place taken by Sergeant Jack Hitchcock, who remained senior NCO in the camp until the end.

It is difficult, in retrospect, to realise that I spent two years in this camp, but contrary to the belief of most people, the monotony of a vegetable existence does not cause time to hang heavily. The days simply pass by, the weeks, the months and in this case even years. This does not mean it was without incident, far from it, but just as at Schlüsselmühle two years earlier, it had become a way of life which had to be accepted. The film and television projection of prisoners of war spending all their time digging escape tunnels is hopelessly removed from the truth. The very *raison d'etre* of a prison camp is the prevention of escape, and it assists a balance of mind on the subject if one reflects that although the German prisoners in England no doubt wished to get back to their own homeland just as much as we did, not a single one made a successful escape back to Germany. In fact the only one to make it at all was the *Luftwaffe* officer Von Werra in 1941, who did not escape from England but from Canada across the border into the then neutral United States. At least the British in Germany made far more attempts and a number were successful, but the proportion in relation to the number of prisoners was still small. This should be borne in mind if my own escapes recorded in this book seem to be very ad hoc; the conditions for escaping with practical expectation of success just did not exist. The only time I even attempted meticulous planning, with Doug Brunger, it came to nought simply because he was returned to *Stalag*, a circumstance beyond our control. And there lies the whole story of any soldier captured by the enemy. From the moment of capture his own life is beyond his own control and lies at the whim of his captors.

I am bound to say my job as interpreter made my prison camp life a great deal more acceptable than working in the sawmills, although I would not have minded that. In many ways the Other Ranks in the *Stalags* were better off than the officers in the *Offlags*. I have no doubt that if anyone had proposed to any British or any other prisoner-of-war officer that he might work he would have indignantly refused it and claimed the right, which existed long before the Convention, to be held captive with full recognition of officer status and no work. In fact, however, we were far better off working — getting outside the camp, meeting others, and in some cases even getting a woman. (Not in my case — pity, but you can't have everything!)

Had I continued working in the normal way, therefore, I would not have minded, but I have to admit the interpreter's job was a lot better. Instead of a life spent entirely in parading each morning, moving out to the sawmills only a few hundred yards away, working, and then returning to the barbed wire, I had a more varied life, going down to the town almost every day, and at least keeping in touch with other people leading a more normal existence.

The fact that Zempelburg was such a small camp was a great

advantage. There was no resident British Officer from the Medical or Dental corps, as applied at *Stalag*, so illnesses or dentistry had to be dealt with by the local civilian professionals. At least once and sometimes twice a week I would take a small party of four or five, accompanied by just one guard, down to the local medico, one Doctor Debuschewitz. Unless the patient was really ill (in which case the doctor came up to the camp, although this was rare), the visit gave the prisoner-of-war patients an opportunity to get out of the camp, and the added pleasure of the doctor's waiting room. Who would normally think of a doctor's waiting room as a desirable place to be? It was in this case. After the austere life in a prison camp, it meant sitting in a room instead of a hut for just an hour or so, with 'normal' people sitting around, and even the presence of women sitting on other chairs gave the waiting room an air of normality long forgotten. The guard would take us into the waiting room where we would wait our normal turn, and remain there while each POW went in to the doctor. I would go in with the first patient and remain there to interpret their ills. I got on well with Dr D. and found that where I did not know a German word, the English word usually sufficed. In fact I learned that most of the English words for ailments were easily understood as they derived more often from the Latin than did the German words.

A similar procedure operated with Fraulein Bleck. Fraulein Bleck was the dentist in Zempelburg, and although toothaches were less common than other ailments, there were usually two or three dental cases in a fortnight which warranted applying to the *Kommandant* for a guard to take us down to Miss Bleck. She was a rather heftily built lady, quite cheerful, and the patients rather liked the idea of having their teeth filled by a lady dentist. The only trouble was that Fraulein Bleck sometimes tried extractions without anaesthetic. To be fair, she usually asked the patient first, and she explained that there were some teeth which an expert could pull out with a jerk without hurting the patient. She was quite right and proved it, but there were one or two unfortunate occasions when it didn't work and the patient was really put through the mill then, as it meant calling her father. Herr Bleck was, I think, about 70 and occupied a small shop opposite his daughter's clinic, where he carried on his own business as dental mechanic. If Fraulein Bleck found a tooth beyond her strength to pull out, she would send for her father, and I was very glad I never had his ministrations. He was a huge man, and would lumber into the room, look at the unhappy patient — who had by this time already suffered the efforts of Fraulein Bleck to tug the tooth out. He would then slowly pick up different sizes of instruments to see which suited him best, while the patient watched him select his chosen instrument of torture.

I liked going to the dentist as Fraulein Bleck had a pretty Polish assistant named Felizia, and I fell for Felizia. The difficulties in the way of getting nearer than standing in the same dentist's surgery were considerable, but by that alchemy which works between young people we understood each other, and when she came to the waiting room door from the surgery to call the next patient and saw there was a prisoner waiting she would excuse herself for a few minutes and go to the toilet one floor down. From the waiting room I too would hear a sudden call of nature, tell the guard where I was going, and pop out for a few minutes. In the nature of the situation nothing more was possible than a quick kiss and cuddle in the angle of the stairs, but it was a pleasant little romance and lightened the day. Chaps in the camp would sometimes come to me to say, 'I'm going to do you a favour — I've got toothache.'

The doctor and dentist were not the only reasons for getting out of the camp for a walk down to the town, as the camp was so small that virtually everything came from Zempelburg — including our daily soup, which was supplied by the two hotels in the town. Let me hasten to correct the instant impression that must surely be given to the reader by the mention of food supplied from hotels. There were two hotels in Zempelburg, Hotel Wiese and Hotel Danziger Hof, and they supplied a couple of cans each to make up enough for a camp of 90 men. I don't know what their customers got, but the soup was no better than at *Stalag*: in fact I can remember several times when Red Cross parcels had been delivered the whole cansful of soup were quietly emptied away. The manner of collecting it was for Jack Hitchcock and myself to go down to the town pulling a two-wheeled cart, with a guard behind us, and bearing yesterday's empty cans, which would be filled in the two hotels. The Hotel Wiese cooked our soup in the boiler used for the washing, and the cookhouse frequently smelt more like a laundry than a kitchen. We would pick up a couple of cans there, then go next door to the Danziger Hof for the next two cans. Of course the guard would be in the kitchen with us in each hotel, but it was still a pleasant little moment of normality, as the kitchen hands were all Polish girls and we got on well with them.

It was natural for the guards to do a bit of shopping of their own in these trips to Zempelburg, and there was one particular grocer's we visited nearly every time, where I got to know two counterhands, both Polish girls. They in turn could contact the male hand there, who worked somewhere inside the building, and who was ready to do a deal occasionally if socks, pullovers or similar clothing were available. A result of this once was that shortly after getting a parcel from home which included a pullover I went in the shop with the guard in apparently good health, but when I came out I had developed a most unfortunate disability in one leg, causing me to limp all the way back to the camp. Once inside my room I was able to take my trousers down and remove the duck which was hanging from a meat hook on my shirt. By good fortune or coincidence we had a tin of peas in that week's Red Cross parcel, and dined that evening off duck and peas, the only such meal I can recall in five years' captivity.

Yet another visit Jack and I paid to the town was the weekly delivery and collection of washing. There were two washer-women living by the side of Zempelburg lake, Frau Bodginski and Frau Kowalski. Jack and I would pull our two-wheeled cart down there with our guard, and spend a pleasant half-hour chatting to Frau Kowalski. We seldom talked much to Bodginski — Kowalski was much more of a motherly soul who liked to talk to us, and she had a 13-year-old-daughter named Katrine, or Katie to us. Sometimes if there was a spare prisoner available in the camp due to time off for minor illnesses or the like, we would have extra help to pull our cart, and on one of these occasions one chap who came with us made an assignation with Frau Bodginski for the next week. He contrived to be available to help with the cart the following week, and when we dropped off half the washing at Bodginski's he remained to help her get it in while Jack and I went on to Kowalski next door. He was only gone about two minutes, but assured us he had performed in that time. We commended him on being swifter than a rabbit.

The guards who accompanied us on these trips varied as humanity varies, but most were reasonable, and in fact one got told off by the police once for standing us a beer in the back room of the grocer's. The regulations required the guard to march a half-dozen paces behind us, but most guards borrowed a revolver instead of a rifle and walked along with us and chatted. This guard duty was not always popular with the guards, as it frequently meant an extra duty for someone who had been on night patrol round the camp.

On the whole, we were not too badly off with the *Kommandants* we got at Zempelburg: most of them were reasonable. But there was one period when we had a swine of a *Kommandant*, and this was the time of the Room With A View.

This particular *Kommandant*, who was in charge of the camp for about eight months, was a very large man, much inclined to leer into my face when he was talking, and spitting as he talked. Unlike most of the guards — and *Kommandants* who, being simply Wehrmacht soldiers, seldom talked Nazi politics — this man was rather fond of pointing to his metal swastika decoration (which was not a campaign decoration, but given for sport) and telling me how proud he was to wear the swastika and how highly he regarded the Fuhrer.

One night, or rather in the early hours of the morning, he roused me out of bed in a barely controlled fury, waving his revolver under my nose and threatening to shoot me if I didn't stop it. I hadn't the faintest idea what he was talking about, but he was in such a temper the situation was clearly dangerous and I had better watch my step. The fellow was almost beside himself in incoherent rage, and it transpired that the police had arrested three prisoners from the camp walking along the pavement in Zempelburg after midnight. It was bad enough for three men to get out, but to be caught by the civilian police when his own guards didn't even know they were out was too much for the *Kommandant*, and he had come barging in to me as someone he could take it out on. This was what I had got to stop apparently. Men getting out. I told him there was no question of stopping

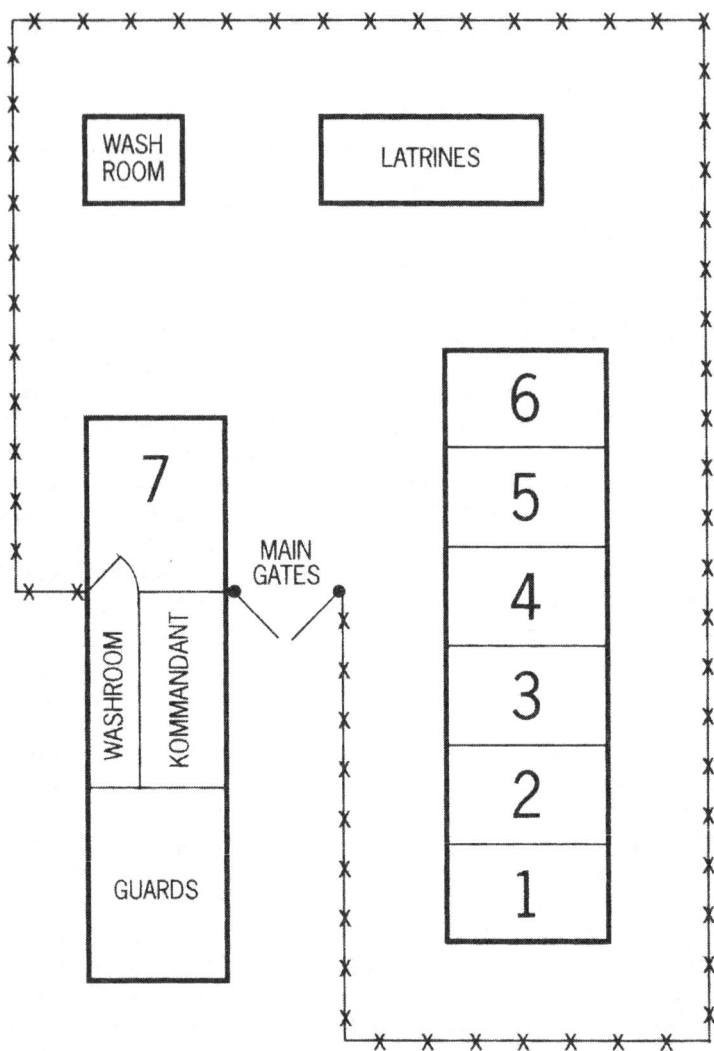

Zempelburg Camp 1943-1945

anyone; it was a soldier's duty to escape, and they were only doing that duty. He pulled me about a bit and raved on, but there was nothing he could do unless he actually shot me, and once that moment of danger had passed I was fairly safe. Eventually he went back to the guardroom to take it out on the guards. I was annoyed about it though. I knew all about this trio getting out that night; it had nothing to do with escaping, they were after women and intended to come back afterwards. What possessed them to walk on the pavement in a dead town in the middle of the night I do not know. Silly buggers, they were asking for trouble, and I was the one that came within an ace of being shot for it.

However we all got our own back on this *Kommandant*, although he never knew it. It all had to do with the Room With a View.

The above diagram shows the construction of the camp — in two long wooden huts, one with six rooms and one with three rooms. The prisoners were housed in seven rooms, six in one hut and one, No.7 room, in the second hut. In this hut the central room was the *Kommandant's* room, and the end room the guard's quarters. The barbed wire was so arranged that the seven prisoners' rooms were within the wire, and the other two rooms outside it. The *Kommandant's* room was slightly smaller than the two rooms on either side, as No.7 room had a little annexe for a washroom.

The dividing wall between the prisoners' washroom and the *Kommandant's* room was a thin partition of matchboarding. Although it looked solid enough from the *Kommandant's* side, the boards did not quite meet, and there were a number of tiny slits between some of the boards which made it possible to peer from the washroom into the *Kommandant's* room.

One evening he brought a woman home to his room and

performed. From then on he conducted an affair with this lady. He liked to see what he was doing, and with the windows masked by black-out shutters he would keep the light on for his gymnastics. There were 14 men in No.7 room and seven slits in the matchboarding, so that each night when the *Kommandant* performed 14 men crept silently into the washroom and composed themselves with two to a slit, the tallest at the top and the smallest crouching down underneath. Only No.7 room could enjoy this entertainment as there had been a spate of escape attempts elsewhere by British prisoners and we were locked in at night, but next day we all got a blow-by-blow account of the previous night's proceedings.

One day some members of No.7 room came to me with a complaint. It seemed that the previous night the *Kommandant* had chosen to roger the lady by the back passage, and for the comfort of the operation had not only used some dripping from a large tin but even commented on its excellent quality. The complaint from my colleagues was that it was *our* fat ration, and he ought to be told about it. They did not of course either expect or intend me to do this — the bastard would probably not only have shot me but No.7 room as well — but prisoners know their food entitlement to a gram and it proved to be quite correct, it *was* our fat ration.

There was no doubt about the superiority of No.7 room during this period. The camp was situated in a fairly barren area of land, with only the woodworks to one side and a cemetery opposite (where we fully expected to end up). With little in the way of scenery, No.7 room was certainly the only Room With A View.

We thought it was our secret, but somebody must have talked, as the senior NCO in the guardroom, an *Unteroffizier*, told me one day all the guards knew about it, but we need not worry, no one would tell the *Kommandant*. He was no more popular with the guards than he was with us. Although it would almost certainly have ended in tragedy if he knew about it, I often thought how nice it would be if that wall fell down and showed the swine there were 14 men watching him all the time.

* * *

It was during the period of tenure of this *Kommandant* that I mislaid one of his guards. I have always been a careless fellow, and in fact there was one awful occasion when I went to *Stalag* to get the Red Cross parcels and left one of the bags behind. I half expected to be lynched for that, but the crime was so heinous they were sorry for me. In the event it only meant the staff room went without Red Cross for a week, and we got the bag back later. Losing an armed guard is a rather more serious matter. It happened in this way.

Jack Hitchcock and I used to go *Stalag* once a week, taking perhaps four or five prisoners who were recalled either for some treatment not available at Zempelburg or perhaps for replacement. We would stay the night at *Stalag* and while the others were getting their treatment or whatever we would collect 90 Red Cross parcels, which went into seven sacks, and catch the train back to Zempelburg.

The train journey was a pleasant break from camp life, as with only one guard and a half-dozen men we would travel in the normal civilian third-class carriage. But neither Jack nor I liked the trip as we both hated the idea of staying a night in *Stalag*. Eventually we got the thing down to a fine art, and by arrangement only one of us would go on alternate weeks — getting up at three in the morning to catch the first train to Nakel, there to change for Thorn, collect the Red Cross from *Stalag* (as well as the latest BBC news from the illicit radio hidden in *Stalag*), and be at Thorn station in time to catch the afternoon train to arrive back at Zempelburg around seven in the evening. Despite the early start and long day for a guard, this was also agreeable to the guards, who disliked a night at *Stalag* barracks as much as we disliked Fort 13.

One morning seven of us assembled at the gate ready for our early start for Thorn, and the *Kommandant* was there to see us safely off. The guard, who was making this trip for the first time, came out and loaded his rifle. (It was a regulation for guards to load their rifles in front of the prisoners each day so that all concerned were in no doubt about it.) The *Kommandant* then gave him the travel voucher and instructions to leave it all to the *Dolmetscher* who was used to this trip and knew what he was doing.

In view of my proven ability to make a balls-up of most jobs as a prisoner so far, the reader may well think this was asking for trouble. In this case however the *Kommandant* was right; I did know what I was doing, and if this unfortunate guard had taken notice of me as he was told to do, he would have saved himself a lot of heartache.

We got to *Stalag* all right and collected the Red Cross in the usual way, chatting to such friends as we met. Then we got our own little party together again, and arrived at Thorn station for the journey back.

We normally got to the station in plenty of time for the train, and checked in the Red Cross bags. These bags were of course no different from any other baggage from the viewpoint of the German railway system, and had to be handed over to the luggage office, entered in the appropriate book, and labelled with destination and amount charged to the army. Since we were used to the procedure it was quite common for Jack or I to jump over the counter into the luggage office and set about labelling the sacks ourselves. The luggage-office personnel were also used to it — after all it saved them some work — and they were always quite content to hear me call out the number of sacks and leave it to me to get them labelled and taken to the luggage van. This also suited us as it meant we kept the precious Red Cross bags under our eyes all the way.

On this occasion we were in reasonable time but not as early as usual, due to the constant stopping of our little group by the guard to make sure we were all there. He was a worrier. It had been bad enough when we all vanished in different directions at *Stalag*, and once he got us all together again he was determined not to lose sight of anyone. When I jumped over the counter and started labelling the bags, with chaps taking them as they were labelled out of the rear door on to the platform and thence down the platform to the luggage van, he kept calling out to keep together, running to and fro to try and keep us in sight. I told him not to worry. The station luggage staff, who were used to us, told him not to worry. To no purpose; he worried. As a result of his interference we only just got the baggage labelled and on the train a couple of minutes before it was due to leave, and then we all piled onto one of the coaches. I called out to him that we were all here, but he wanted to make sure no one was still in the luggage hall and ran back. He got back to the platform just in time to see the train steaming out with me leaning out of a window and waving to him.

There was no question of using the occasion for making a break, that just wasn't on. There was nothing for it but to make the whole return journey on our own. We got to Nakel, got out of the train and went to the guard's van to get our Red Cross. This was also standard practice: we simply collared one of the platform trucks, loaded the sacks on to it and trundled across to the platform for the local train to Konitz. This was the first time anybody queried our movements. An officer leaning out of the train we had arrived in asked me as I passed him with the truck where our guard was, as he didn't see one. I said we had started with one, but he missed the train, but not to worry as we knew where we were going. He said he had never heard of such a thing, and as his train started he called out that someone, anyone, should take charge of these prisoners. No one took any notice.

We loaded our Red Cross onto the Konitz train and in due course arrived at Zempelburg. The *Kommandant* was waiting on the platform; he did not normally bother to meet us, so perhaps he had a little worry of his own about his guard. As we got down from the train, the others automatically made for the Red Cross to unload it, and the *Kommandant* asked me where the guard was. I said we had left him behind in Thorn. He chose to be amused, and very unnatural was this fellow when he was amused.

'Ha, ha, *Dolmetscher*, that is your little joke. But all the same where is he?'

I assured him it was no joke; we had travelled all the way from Thorn with no guard, changing trains on the way. As the penny dropped his face dropped also, much like a comic double-take in a film, and certainly more comical to see than his original untypical *bonhomie*.

I was not at all surprised when he suggested that it was my fault, as I should have looked after the fellow, but this was no more than the natural reaction of a man of his nature to look for someone handy to blame, and required no answer from me. He knew perfectly well the guard was supposed to be guarding us, not the other way round.

The guard did not return to the camp. Whether this was no more than a normal replacement or whether the poor chap went to the penal battalion I never knew. I rather think nothing much happened to him; this was one instance where the *Kommandant* would have made no protest, and quite possibly even supported his guard. Commanders of prison camps, whether officers or NCOs may or may not have known any American phrases, but they knew well enough where the buck stopped.

It was also during this *Kommandant's* reign that at long, long last, the war showed signs of turning from constant German victories to Allied successes, and with it the thought that we might after all survive long enough to get home before the time to draw our old-age pensions. The Russian victory at Stalingrad had come and gone, but we were more interested in the western end of the war. The British victory at Alamein had also long since come and gone, but we were (like many others elsewhere) a little wary of British victories in Libya: they had so far only meant advances to be followed by retreats back to and beyond the start line. Now however the war in the western desert had really shown some Allied dividends, and not before time.

The Eighth Army had pursued the Germans and Italians back to Tunisia, Americans together with the British First Army had landed in North Africa, and in May 1943 came the first really large German capitulation at Tunis. I had been to *Stalag* that week, and came back with the griff from the hidden radio in Fort 13. Knowing my audience, I had taken a lot of it down, and read it out to the camp when I got back to Zempelburg. It was the most heartening war news we had had so far, and it really lightened the spirits of the whole camp. As we had already been prisoners for three years we were not too keen on Churchill's comment that it was not the end, or even the beginning of the end, but only the end of the beginning — but never mind, it began to look as though, to quote one prisoner, we had broken the back of our term of captivity.

We were not without news of the war as it progressed. As *Dolmetscher* I got an official issue of the national newspaper, the *Volkischer Beobachter*. This was rather like the *Daily Express* in format, but unlike that paper was not one of a number of national newspapers available to a democratic public. Nazi Germany was a dictatorship, and the *Beobachter* had been founded by the Minister of Propaganda, Dr Goebbels, as a vehicle for disseminating such news as was appropriate for the public to read, and of course slanted in a similarly appropriate manner. I used to read this out each day, but although it was useful to keep in touch with main events, nobody really believed it all, even when events proved they were telling the truth. This of course is why no one believed the boy who cried wolf; if you habitually tell lies how can anyone sift the wheat from the chaff?

Although the *Beobachter* was my only official newspaper, I also usually got a copy of the local *Zeitung* given to me either by a guard or one of the Poles. This of course contained the same official communiqués, but the more local news gave a better picture of the situation as it was affecting the population, and there was no doubt that Germany was now on the defensive.

There came a glorious news day for me personally when Italy capitulated. This was headline news in the *Volkischer Beobachter*, and the camp was overjoyed when I showed them the paper. It was not just rumour this time, it was even acknowledged by the Nazis. The point of particular pleasure for me in this was that I had spent over three years being asked each day for news from the German paper, and more often than not it was either German victory or at the least something detrimental to the Allies — and particularly to England, which had been in the war all along. At last there was something heavily in our favour for me to read out, and in the German paper too! I was most gratified.

The camp was also gratified by an action of an Austrian at Ingbau Hellmann where everybody worked. This fellow, one Herr Hammer, was not there every day, and I am not sure whether he was really an employee. If so, he was probably a traveller for the firm. He did not have anything to do with the prisoners, and his only two claims for notice were (a) a strong loyalty to the Nazis, and (b) the fact that he was a brother to Ernestine Hammer, a prett, plump Austrian girl who worked in the office, and whose occasional appearances in the factory led to some interesting discussion among the prisoners.

Herr Hammer demonstrated his loyalty by wearing a neat and expensive-looking enamelled badge with three flags branching out from it: those of Germany, Italy and Japan, the Axis powers. After the capitulation of Italy he still wore his badge, but had broken off the flag of Italy, which, as the *Beobachter* screamed in its headlines, had betrayed the Axis. No doubt if the Italian people knew Hammer had removed their flag from his badge, they would have borne it bravely.

Not long after this our large and spitting *Kommandant* departed, and his place was taken by *Unteroffizier* Seidel, who was to remain with us for a year and achieve the impossible — a popularity with the prisoners. Whether a *Kommandant* was 'good' or 'bad' he was an enemy; he could easily be hated, or, if a just man, might achieve recognition as 'fair', but that was about the limit of it. He could never be popular. But Seidel managed this; not by ingratiating himself — that would never have worked

— but simply by being himself, a reasonable human being. This was so rare among *Kommandants* that when Seidel left us, a year later, there was a collection of precious cigarettes for him, something unknown in my experience of prisoner-of-war camps.

Prison camp life for a long-term prisoner of war tends to be seen in *Kommandant* terms rather than in calendar years, rather like royal reigns in English history, and with Seidel we were entering a new year of 1943/44.

8

A Plane in the Night

Not long after Seidel's acquisition of the *Kommandant's* job in September 1943 we lost a member of the staff room, Jack our medical orderly. The manner of his going was an event of astonishment that made us all green with envy.

One evening I was called to the *Kommandant's* office and told to bring the Sani with me. This was another of those instances where the German word was used more than our own; the German word for medical orderly is *Sanitater*, and Jack was known as the Sani. He was a quiet man, older than most of us, and efficient at this job. It was no surprise for him to be called to the German office as he attended minor cuts and abrasions for the Germans as well as for ourselves.

This time however he was wanted for something different, a little news. There was to be a repatriation of men 'on the Commission'. The phrase referred to the international Red Cross Commission with whom were registered badly wounded prisoners or any that became sufficiently ill in captivity to warrant inclusion on the Commission list, and this list also included registered first-aid personnel. Jack was a regimental first-aid orderly, and therefore on the list.

It so happened we were due to go to *Stalag* for Red Cross next day, and Jack was to go with the party, stay a night at Stalag, entrain with others the following morning for Danzig and then board a Swedish Red Cross ship for Stockholm and Newcastle. He would be in England in a few days.

We had always known there was a Red Cross Commission and that men on it were supposed to be repatriated, but as the years passed and nothing happened we had long since given up any thought that anyone would actually be repatriated while the war was still on. So when Jack came back into the staff room it was not easy for anyone to believe this was really happening; here we were 1,000 miles from England and someone was actually packing a bag to go home! We had of course often discussed our own likely reaction to the news of going home, presumably when the war was won and not before, and we all assumed joy abounding, getting drunk and generally making merry. Maybe we would be like that, but it didn't apply to Jack. He showed no more emotion than when attending to patients, which was none at all. Nevertheless there it was, a prisoner of war inside the barbed wire, with guards patrolling outside it, and in a week he would be home. It was difficult to grasp, especially as it was unexpected, but it was there right enough, and I think we all wished we had joined the Medical Corps. It proved to be the only repatriation in the whole war, and as it reached into the past it faded in our memories, but it had been an event to lift the spirits with its reminder that prisoners of war were not entirely forgotten.

In due course we received a replacement, a Scotsman who did not remain very long. He in turn was replaced by 'Spud' Taylor, a medical orderly from my own regiment, who became our Sani at Zempelburg for the rest of the war. Spud was younger and more loquacious than Jack had been, but just as good at his job, and we were glad to have him.

By this time we had learned to make our own wine, if wine it can be called. It was found that a packet of raisins — or if not available, prunes — would produce a beverage which, if not exactly Chateau d'Yquem, was at least alcoholic. Of course, we did not have yeast, but a little trading with the Poles produced it, and there was no difficulty in hiding the operation. We simply obtained a milk churn, threw in our raisins, or more often prunes, added the yeast, and left it until required.

One day around Christmas I went into one of the rooms (No.7 room again, I think), and two of the chipped metal mugs we all had were thrust at me. I took them both, one in each hand, and to show my appreciation of this hospitality took a swig from each. It tasted vile, but as far as I was concerned all this home-made wine tasted the same, except that it was a bit worse with prunes than with raisins. I saw nothing special about this particular brew. There obviously was something special, however, as the room was quiet for a moment, and they looked at me. Someone said, 'He's tougher than he looks,' and asked if I felt anything. I said no and that I was fine. I could see I had gone up in everyone's estimation, so presumably this wine was a little stronger than usual, although I didn't notice it — at least not immediately.

Suddenly I felt very ill and had to rush out and vomit uncontrollably. My stock went down again: clearly I was not so tough after all. I was in good company; half the camp was ill, as well as a couple of guards who had been unwise enough to taste the prisoners' illicit brew.

It seemed that this particular vintage was the usual simple mixture of water, prunes and yeast, but with one interesting addition. Apparently someone in the room had heard, read or simply invented the idea that boot polish had an alcoholic content, and having recently received a tin of polish in his personal home parcel, had stirred in a complete tin of Cherry Blossom boot-blacking. (I offer the idea free to home-made wine producers for adding that certain *je ne sais quoi*.)

It was a pity I was ill, as I might otherwise have basked in the unusual role of tough guy. I suppose my stomach, which must have become resistant to coping with unusual concoctions in the war years, felt it was time to object when I sent down boot polish.

Time moved on into the spring of 1944, and we received an inspection visit from a General, no less. I went round the camp with him, and at one point asked him if he would be good enough to speak a little louder as I was fairly deaf. He said he was just about to tell me to open my mouth more as he was also deaf, and we completed the inspection in loud tones. In such a small camp there was not much for him to inspect, but at the end of it he suddenly turned on me and asked my rank. I told him I was a *Schütze*. (By the chance of language this was more accurate than many other translations. In the British army the unranked soldier is normally called a Private, except in special regiments where he may be called a Gunner, Sapper, Guardsman or Rifleman. In the German army the word for a private soldier is *Schütze* or Rifleman.)

The General then told Seidel there was no justification for keeping a private soldier in the camp as interpreter, and he should arrange for me to go out to work. He then departed, leaving Seidel as unhappy with this dictum as I was.

The fact was that Seidel did not want to lose his *Dolmetscher*. I was not only useful in that role, and in fact had sometimes written his official letters for him, but the camp prisoner staff had already been reduced to three, and it needed at least two and sometimes three to lug the cart down to Zempelburg to collect soup, washing and anything else that might be required. Also it was clear someone would be needed to take the sick or dental party down.

Nor was this all. Pollvogts, the *Betriebmeister*, and most of the camp did not relish the idea of me working in the factory. My propensity for carelessness was almost a byword, and the thought of me being let loose among the many kinds of powered saws was enough to chill the blood.

It was the *Betriebsmeister* who came up with the solution. Seidel could keep me in the camp for the morning, which included the time appropriate for going down to the town, and I would have a light job in the office in the afternoon. My job was to be assistant to one Herr Hackemann, and I really could find no grounds for complaint at all. Considering I had briefly faced the awful prospect of regular work, I had truly fallen on my feet.

Hackemann had an office of his own in the office block and was responsible for stores. My own job with him was to be the collection of the *Zetteln* sent in from the factory each day. A *zettel* is simply a slip of paper, or chitty, and anyone in the factory requiring anything from the stores — a bag of nails, a screwdriver or whatever — and whether German, Pole or prisoner, would obtain a *Zettel* from his foreman and present this to the storekeeper. This *Zettel* in due course found its way to Hackemann's office, where from now on Hackemann's new assistant would sort them out and enter them in the appropriate book. For this purpose I was given a desk in Hackemann's office immediately opposite the typist's office, which was occupied by the delectable Fraulein Ernestine Hammer.

Herr Hackemann was absent more often than present, although he usually contrived to be there at three o'clock in the afternoon. This was the time of the German broadcast of the War Communiqué, and Hackemann had the only radio in the building. At three therefore, the senior office staff gathered in what quickly became regarded as 'my' office to listen to the broadcast.

On my very first day Hackemann explained my job, stayed to listen to the three o'clock news, and departed. Almost immediately Ernstl Hammer appeared in my office to ask if I knew anything about repairing typewriters, as hers had broken down. I accompanied her across the corridor and looked at the recalcitrant typewriter. I tinkered about a bit (there was of course nothing wrong with it), got it going, and stayed for a little dalliance with Ernstl. Thus our business relationship was established from the word go, but although we understood each other perfectly it was destined to be platonic.

The day after the typewriter repair, and after the departure of Hackemann, she thought she saw a mouse in her room — this rodent having apparently disappeared through the door inside her room. This door led to the darkroom, Ingbau Hellmann being right up-to-date and photocopying their documents, a rather more cumbersome process at that early stage which required actual development of film.

I was quite pleased to go and look for this elusive mouse, and she accompanied me into the darkroom to look for it. She was just putting her hand out to shut the door when the door to her office was flung open by Pollvogts who had brought some prints for development. After that we were both too frightened to take any risk inside the office. If we were caught in any sexual relationship it would mean Graudenz for me, and for her at least ten years in prison and perhaps execution. This is not an exaggeration. Cases appeared in the newspapers from time to time of the fate of German women caught sullying their Aryan blood by association with prisoners of war or slave labourers. So platonic it had to be; but it was friendship, and just like a meeting with Felizia at the dentist, added a little normality to an otherwise monastic existence.

Ernstl had a friend Gisela who sometimes met her at the works, and when she once took Gisela into the works to show her round Les Alsop fell for her at once. In POW life there is no time for finesse, and he told me that night that he wished to tell Ernstl he was in love with her friend and wanted an arrangement to meet after dark. It would mean getting through the wire, which was of course guarded, and afterwards getting back again, but that would be his problem. I was just to arrange it.

Next day I told Ernstl of this soul-love at a distance, and asked her if we could arrange a foursome one night. It meant long negotiations over some weeks, as Ernstl did not see her friend every day and with two of the parties not in contact the whole thing required determination to pursue it at all. Eventually an arrangement was made, but at the last minute Ernstl told me she was not prepared to risk it. I do not blame her, and I think perhaps I felt a little relieved myself. It probably sounds a bit priggish, but I felt that if you were going to make a break-out it ought to be with at least the intent to make a genuine break, even if it afterwards failed, and much as I wanted to be alone with the desirable Hammer I was not too happy with the idea of risking my neck for a wire-passage both ways just for a grind. There was a least one case of a prisoner being shot dead on the wire and given a full scale funeral as an escaper, although he had in fact been coming *in* after an amatory exploit.

Gisela however was prepared to keep the appointment, and Les, somewhat to my surprise, actually made it. He got through the wire both ways, and despite a narrow escape on the return, having virtually to launch himself through the wire just ahead of the guard's turn of the corner, completed the whole thing successfully. Since Les was quite a handsome man it was generally felt in the camp that Gisela had done well for herself, but neither party was prepared to risk it again. Gisela was really taking the greater risk; she was a German and would have got the chop if caught.

My job proved to be even easier than it was at the start. Hackemann had fallen well behind in dealing with his *Zetteln*; there was quite a pile to start with, but the job was easy enough, and I quite soon got it down to a situation of working only a couple of hours a day. The job proved to be of some use to the camp, as I now heard the communiqué as it was issued each day, so we had the up-to-date news in the camp within minutes of the broadcast. All I had to do was go to the latrine (oh yes, the term latrine rumour is justified, it is *the* source of news) and any interesting news in the communiqué was round the workplace within minutes.

There was one under-manager in the office who never failed to attend Hackemann's office for the news broadcast, and one day he stayed after the broadcast to tell me he was beginning to think the Allied talk of an invasion of Europe was bluff, as we were now into summer and nothing seemed to be happening. At all events, if there was to be an invasion it would not be now, as the weather was against it. Although this was no more than a passing comment on the day's news, or in this case lack of it, I remember this particular remark very well. The date was 5 June 1944, and the next day was D day.

The morning of D day passed normally enough, except that there were general rumours that the Germans were claiming some success in France at having destroyed some sort of parachute drop. At three o'clock I was in 'my' office and knew immediately something was afoot: the communiqué was such a standard item that normally only one or two of the senior office came in to listen to it, but this time they all came. The communiqué did not in fact announce the invasion, but only that the British and Americans had dropped parachute troops in France. I would have liked a clear announcement of the invasion to have the pleasure of passing on, but this was clear enough. If we had dropped parachute troops we meant to invade (of course we had already done so hours ago, but the news was not yet broadcast), and I made for the latrine to pass on the news.

Afterwards I wandered round the works, where all the Poles and prisoners were as cheerful as the Germans were solemn, and behind one of the piles of Bretter I came across an old man, one of the oldest Poles on the job. He was sitting all on his own on the ground with his back against the wood pile, crying his eyes out. I asked him what was the matter, didn't he know the rest of his friends were all happy today? He said he was crying from happiness as he had always known Koorkill (Churchill) would not let them down. He had trusted in Koorkill for five years, since Poland had been occupied in 1939, and he always knew the invasion would come because Koorkill was a man of his word, and Poland would soon be free. Alas, poor Poland.

Only a couple of weeks after D Day we got our own radio. This project had been in hand some time, and involved much bargaining with Poles for valves and other bits and pieces. My own mucker Phin played a notable part in this, as he was a member of a tobacco family and from time to time received extra parcels of cigarettes, which he generously gave out, or in this case exchanged for valves. Our radio was a very primitive affair of only two valves, but we could get England on it, and for security it was arranged that it would be available only to the Staff room, and even then only to the Staff, which meant excluding Phin. We buried it under the floor of the tiny medical room, and came the greatest day when Jack, Spud and I shut the door, opened our trapdoors, adjusted the headphones and prepared to hear the BBC.

After four years as a prisoner in enemy hands, the very first broadcast I heard direct from England was exactly right for the occasion. It was not a news broadcast. We had tuned in during a radio film programme, and at precisely that moment the BBC broadcast part of the sound track of a new film. It was Laurence Olivier's production of *Henry V*, and at exactly the moment we tuned in the programme presenter starting running his chosen excerpt from the film. It was the Harfleur speech, 'Once more unto the breach, dear friends...' The heavy, perhaps hammy, patriotism in this address might not be as much in vogue today as in Shakespeare's time, or for that matter in the early 1930s when I was kept in at school for not learning the passage for homework, but after four years' captivity — and with the D Day landings only a week earlier — it fitted our mood, and I was moved by it.

Our early euphoria at the D Day landings gave way to depression in the weeks that followed. The invasion had been longed for as the long-awaited second front that would bring a speedy end to the war, but after the initial landings the Allies seemed to have settled down in the bridgehead, with no sign of the great dash into Germany we had all expected. The 1914 war had been fought in trenches well to the east of the present Allied landing front, and that one had taken four years. Were we really to stay here for years to come, to finally move over to the cemetery across the road?

For my own part, I thought more and more of my home town, London, and felt not only that I wanted to get back, but specifically to do so before the war ended. Escape was currently out of the question, as the Germans had become rather trigger-happy where escapers were concerned, and in fact had stated bluntly in posters put up in all the camps that escapers would be shot if caught in so-called 'death-zones'. These zones seemed to cover the greater part of Germany and German-occupied territory. The heading to this poster was 'Escaping is no longer a sport,' and it will be remembered by most POWs who were in German hands at that time. One has to admit they had a point — it had been regarded as something of a sport.

How else to get back before the war was over? The Russians seemed to be bogged down on the other side of the Vistula, but at least they were in Poland and nearer than the Western Allies. Perhaps they might get a move on and get close enough to escape to the Russian troops. What then? Would one be repatriated via Moscow, or would the Russians simply leave such flotsam to find their own way back via the Black Sea? Or shoot you? Perhaps after all the British and Americans would move their backsides and get close enough to reach them, although this seemed hardly likely.

Well, never mind. Perhaps some opportunity as yet unforeseen might present itself. It would certainly be at least a mental mark to aim at, even if it proved no more than academic — the possibility of being back in London before the war ended. Piccadilly Circus, the centre of the West End. That would be the place to be on the day the war ended. Oh well, it cost nothing to dream dreams.

Then at last the Allies broke out of the bridgehead and started a dash through France and Belgium even faster than the original German *Blitzkreig*. We were of course delighted with this, but this time we had problems nearer home to engage our attention.

Bugs.

It had been lice at Rittel, fleas at Schlüsselmühle, and now it was bugs at Zempelburg. The things were all over the huts and in every crevice of the woodwork and the beds. The Allies did not pursue the retreating Germans in France with more determination than we pursued the bugs, but it was a battle we could not win, and we were bitten unmercifully.

Eventually authority was persuaded to take some notice, and we were all moved out to a new hut which Hellman had built next to our camp apparently as some sort of village hall. We all slept on the floor of this hall for a week or so while our huts were fumigated with sulphur. It is a period I remember chiefly for the daily news in the *Volkischer Beobachter* at the time. The July plot on Hitler's life had failed, and while we were being de-bugged, the poor devils who had taken part were being tried in a People's Court where the verdict was pre-ordained. One might feel that sympathy is out of place for these Generals who had taken an enthusiastic part in Hitler's war until it was clear he was not going to win it; but their number did include some genuine idealists, and even those who had seen the light a bit late were at least trying to do something to stop the holocaust. They were all hanged on piano wire and cine-film taken of their death agonies to amuse Hitler in his leisure moments.

We returned to our sulphurous but now happily bug-free huts in the compound, but the short sojourn in the now adjacent new hut gave me an idea. The new building had a small stage — could we use this to stage some form of entertainment like the concert party of three years ago?

Permission was obtained from the Kommandant, blankets were sacrificed to rig up curtains, scripts were written and rehearsed, and we had a show. Just one. It was acceptable enough and provided a welcome break in life's monotony, but it was 1944: we had been prisoners for four years and simply could not work up much enthusiasm for the entertainment. This, however, led to the famous public production of Snow White and the Seven Dwarfs.

It started with Katrina, the 13-year-old daughter of Frau Kowalski, our washerwoman by the Zempelburg lake. The next time Jack and I went with our guard to collect the washing, Katrina asked me if we would do her school a favour. They had rehearsed a play and had been given permission to stage it in the new hut next to our camp, but they had no stage facilities other than the little stage itself. The whole town knew we had given a POW show of our own, and the favour requested was to use our blanket curtains. Rather than putting them back on our beds, would we please leave them up until the weekend so that the school could use them for this school play? Of course we said yes and thought no more about it.

On the following Sunday however, Jack and I asked the Kommandant's permission to go outside the wire to the hut next door to retrieve our blankets, and this being given, we passed out of the gate to the next door hut. Our real intention, of course, was to make sure the children and their teachers did not tear or cut these blankets in any way; hang it all, we had to sleep on them.

The school production, whatever it was, had been scheduled for Sunday afternoon, and sure enough on Sunday chairs were ranged in lines in the main floor of the hut, and our blanket curtains were drawn. Jack and I went behind the curtains and almost immediately the audience began to arrive. Looking through the centre of the curtains we could see it was just the gathering you would expect, clearly a lot of fond mothers, many with small children. At around the same time children began arriving behind the stage, Katrina among them. The average age of the children was around six or seven, obviously the youngest class, and Katrina was apparently some sort of helper from an older class. Where were the teachers? Katrina said they were supposed to be there to supervise the show, but there was only a bunch of infants and Katrina — no teacher.

It was well beyond the scheduled starting time and the audience was getting restless, and the small children were becoming clamourous and noisy. Katrina begged me to get something started, and it was only at this point I learned the title of the entertainment: *Schneewittchen [Snow White]*.

I marshalled these unknown but trusting children onto the stage, Jack and I walked back with the two halves of curtain, and the great show began. Against all the odds, given such a beginning, it went quite well. I did not of course have any prompt script, but the children had clearly been well-rehearsed and started off in fine fettle. One little girl was the wicked queen and I can remember to this day her lines: *'Spieglein, spieglein auf der Wand, wer ist die schoenst im ganzen Land?'* ('Mirror, mirror on the wall, who is the fairest of them all?') Katrina gave me a sign when that particular scene was ended and Jack and I drew the curtains. Then, with Katrina's instructions, we managed to set the stage for the next scene. This had a table in the centre with seven little stools and seven little bowls and spoons. It was this scene which gave a warning that all might not go as smoothly as the first scene.

The dwarfs marched on, each with a lantern, the last a tot so small the lamp was almost as big as its bearer. This was not of course the Disney version, but there followed some song and then they all sat down at the table. Enter Snow White. I have of course long forgotten her line, but it was something like, 'What have we here — seven dwarfs?' No reply. Nothing. The dwarfs did not even look in her direction. Some fond mother had provided these seven bowls with jelly, and the dwarfs were much too busy spooning this treat to waste time on Snow White. She tried several times with, 'What have we here?', but the heroine and the whole audience had to wait until the last scrap of jelly had been spooned by the last dwarf. The scene continued with increasing chaos but at last, mercifully, it was at an end and Jack and I drew the curtains.

It took a little time to clear the stage and set the next scene, and meanwhile out front there was an ominous rise in the noise level. I saw through the chink in the curtains that the smallest tots were running about and shouting, encouraged by one special horror who kept running up to the stage and poking his finger through a hole in the blanket. I waited with my face near the hole and next time he thrust his finger through I bit it. He gave a loud yell and ran screaming to his mother, who simply slapped him. The old cures are the best.

Behind the curtains the production was disintegrating. Two of the dwarfs were fighting, one little girl came up to me and having taken her clothes off, expected me to dress her (I remember feeling embarrassed because I had no idea how to dress a little girl). There was a general milling about as the children were struggling to remember what they were supposed to do next. By this time Jack and I were stripped to the waist and sweating freely. Katrina explained the next scene was some sort of crowd scene, and Jack and I stood with our backs to our halves of the curtain trying to marshal them all into some semblance of order when the whole problem was solved. With an accompanying roar from the audience our whole makeshift system of curtains fell down and the audience was treated to the spectacle of two enemy soldiers marshalling their little darlings into a group on the stage.

It was of course the end of the (literal) pantomime. Somehow audience and cast dispersed and Jack and I were left with an empty stage and some torn blankets. The astonishing thing is that all this took place in a hut right next to the camp, but neither guards nor prisoners had any idea that a great production of *Snow White* was literally a few yards away. I found next time I went into the village for supplies that the fame of the performance had spread through Zempelberg, but I never found out what had happened to the teachers.

It was not long after this that we were overflown by a ghost aeroplane. It was the extraordinary incident of the Plane in the Night. Were it not for the fact that I am aware the incident could be confirmed by many thousands of POWs who survived Stalag XXA, it might sound a little far-fetched to say the least. It really had to do with the famous German iron discipline.

It was natural from our early capture to find the camp had a large proportion of regular soldiers, and it was always their opinion that discipline in the British army was at least as strict, and perhaps stricter, than that appertaining in the German army. Having seen both, I am inclined to agree, but it depends what is meant by the word. In the German army the rigidity of the discipline was based on unquestioning obedience to orders — *Befehl von Oben* — superior orders. The world became used to the answers given at the Nuremburg trials that atrocities were committed through superior orders, but although humanity may well take that as no excuse for the unmentionable abominations committed by the SS and SD, it is a fact that throughout the German army superior orders were not to be questioned. There can surely be no doubt that a reasonable *Kommandant* like

Seidel, or any other normal thinking man, would not have tried to inflict on the prisoners the incident of the Plane in the Night unless it had been by superior orders.

It had to do with an attempt to recruit British prisoners of war into the German army. Fighting for the Germans on the Eastern Front were a number of voluntary divisions drawn from pro-Nazis in the occupied countries — as for instance Leon Degrelle's Belgian SS division, the 'Viking' division drawn from Scandinavia, and some Vichy French. An attempt had been made early in the war to form an English unit, to be known as the British Free Corps, but although in 1940 the Germans had found a literal handful of traitors to form the nucleus of it, the BFC was a dismal failure. We knew of its existence, but it was so remote that it was not even a subject for occasional discussion. In the late summer of 1944, however, it was brought to our notice in an amusing, if startling, fashion.

One morning a little before Reveille the *Unteroffizier*, who was Seidel's second-in-command, came into the billet and woke me up. I slept in a top bunk, and as I am a sound sleeper by the time he had wakened me the whole of the room was awake.

I am never at my best early in the morning (who is?) and I hung my head over the top of the bunk and looked at him blearily. He was holding a paper in his hand, and after he had repeated himself about half-a-dozen times I vaguely grasped that he was asking me to translate it. I suppose I was looking at him pretty dully, for he finally held it in front of my nose and loudly demanded a translation.

It proved to be a short pamphlet printed in English, and ostensibly written by an Englishman since it was signed 'The British Free Corps'. It exhorted the reader to join the Corps, and tabulated the Corps' objects, which were, roughly, to cease being Germany's enemy, to don German uniform and fight the Russians, and to assist in throwing all the Jews and plutocrats out of England. The 'Jews and Plutocrats' was a favourite phrase of the Germans and crept into most articles or speeches that touched on England.

I thought that the *Unteroffizier* must surely know what the pamphlet was all about since it was obviously German in origin, and said as much, but he insisted on a translation and, on getting it, told us that it was one of a number that had been dropped on the camp by a British aeroplane during the night. Had we not heard the aeroplane?

Most emphatically we had not.

He assured us, however, that such was the case, and then delivered himself of the following amazing speech in the parrot-like tones of one who has learned something by heart:

'These pamphlets were dropped by a British plane during the night. Since they were in English I asked for a translation in case they were enemy propaganda, in which case of course they would have been confiscated. However as there is nothing in them prejudicial to Germany, I shall leave them where they are and you can pick them up and read them.'

And from that he would not budge. He obviously felt rather embarrassed about it and left us to work it out for ourselves.

We pulled on our trousers and went out to see the pamphlets that had been 'dropped' by a (silent) British plane. They were there all right. The pilot of the plane must have been dropping pamphlets from birth, for not a single one had fallen outside the wire of our small compound. Better still, they were grouped conveniently round the door. And, in order to ensure that none blew away, each had a stone on it to keep it flat on the ground!

Needless to say none of them was touched and about midday

the *Unteroffizier* came in himself and collected them all up. We never referred to it again, and I think he was thankful that we didn't.

We subsequently found that during that week precisely the same comedy was enacted in almost every other camp in the *Stalag*. In some cases the pamphlets were dropped by the ghost aeroplane in the compounds of farm working parties of ten or twelve men, where the compound was only a few yards square; and in *Stalag* they were not only dropped on the circular path trodden by the prisoners in their daily exercise but, like our own case, had stones on them to keep them down until 'found'. In all cases the same story of the 'British plane in the night' was rigidity adhered to. In the whole operation, embracing thousands of British prisoners of war in this *Stalag* alone (was it done in other *Stalags* I wonder?), there was not a single convert, nor was it treated anywhere with anything but the contempt it deserved.

This order must have come from fairly high up to have been obeyed so universally in the *Stalag*, but before we smile too much at what seems monumental naivety it is as well to remember that this same unquestioning obedience to orders produced an army that occupied most of Europe and held out against superior forces for six years.

I would like to have kept one of those pamphlets as a souvenir, but we British have our own unquestioning forms of rigidity at times; no orders were issued, the matter was not discussed, but no one touched a single one of the pamphlets.

* * *

Time moved on, and with it Kommandant Seidel, clutching his present of cigarettes from the prisoners. There were some who felt it wrong to give cigarettes to a hated enemy, but the British

— while ever ready to spring to arms to oppose aggressors — are very bad at hating them, and the consensus of opinion was that Seidel had been a good and fair *Kommandant*. So he got his cigarettes.

He was replaced by Kommandant Moeller, who proved to be as reasonable as Seidel, and was to be our last *Kommandant*. Moeller was an older man, and although he did his duty in commanding the guards and carrying out his own orders vis-à-vis his prisoners (such as the recent *Stalag* order to take away our trousers at night as an extra anti-escape measure), his heart was not in it. He was quite simply fed up with the war, which he knew perfectly well was lost, and the sooner it was over the better.

The war was now going badly for Germany with the Western Allies just west of the Rhine, and the Russians poised the other side of the Vistula. But there, incredibly, it seemed to us, they all stopped. The Warsaw uprising in August produced no matching advance by the Red Army (for reasons perhaps more easily understood by prisoners in Poland, in constant contact with the Poles, than in, say, Bournemouth), while in the west the September attempt to cross the lower Rhine through an airborne assault on Arnhem had come to nought, and the British and American armies seemed to settle down for the winter.

There was no doubt about the effect of the war on Germany. During the last quarter of 1944 the average age of the guards went up considerably as replacements were men called up in their fifties. Even their arms got older, as the standard issue of German rifles was withdrawn from prison camp guards and they were issued with ancient French rifles, which were either from the Franco-Prussian War of 1870, or at the least well prior to the 1914 war. Hermann got such a rifle.

Hermann was my very own guard that autumn. As I have

already mentioned, the job of guarding me when I went to the town with a party for the doctor or some similar errand, was not popular. It was easy enough and such guards were usually quite relaxed and friendly, but it was an extra duty, and best avoided. The Hermanns of this world are to be found in every conscripted army in the world: the awkward member of the squad. Hermann was a simple soul; to put it bluntly he was not really all there. He was very tall, about six foot three, and when he slung his pre-historic extra-long French rifle on his shoulder, topped by a two-foot-long sword bayonet, he looked fearsome. He could also be damn dangerous when handling this weapon.

The first time he was given the guard job to accompany me to the town, Moeller stood with him to get him launched. Hermann took the rifle in hand to load it. Instead of holding it at the port in the normal way for loading, he just could not manage to keep his mind on what both hands were doing at the same time. As he inserted the three-round clip into the magazine, he waved the muzzle of the rifle across the stomachs of both Moeller and me. (A three-round clip — that shows how old these rifles were!)

Moeller stood fast, but this was too much for me. I took the rifle off him — with no protest from either Hermann or Moeller — inserted the clip, closed it, then held out my hand for the bayonet. He glanced at Moeller, who nodded, and thankfully handed it to me. I clipped it on, and handed it back to him. It went against the grain to actually load a rifle for an enemy to guard me with, but this fellow was a menace. Thereafter it became practice for me to load for him, and fix the bayonet he somehow could never manage to fit into its socket.

Hermann was not popular with his fellow guards as he had very dirty habits, but this was only because he was simple-minded, and should not have been in the army at all. He was not all alone; his kind could be found in the British or any other army in wartime.

Eventually Hermann vanished, and was later reported as having been seen crawling on his hands and knees in the punishment battalion. We were sorry when we heard this, but only momentarily, as we had troubles of our own by this time. The Red Cross parcels had stopped, and we were now reliant on the slops delivered in the name of soup from the Hotels Wiese and Danziger Hof once a day. Even the local deals for eggs were now few and far between, as our own possessions of socks and pullovers had dwindled to personal minimums.

As we approached Christmas 1944 we acquired a supply of flour. I cannot remember where this came from, but it was the only item in the camp apart from the soup, and since there is nothing much one can do with flour on its own, we simply mixed it with water and made pancakes with it. I am still a dab hand at tossing a pancake.

I also acquired transport at this time. The management of Ingbau Hellman bought a second-hand electric truck from somewhere, found they had no use for it after all, and offered it to Moeller to collect his bits and pieces from the town. I was the only one to use it.

Once a day I went to the works and collected the truck. It was reminiscent of the electric trucks used on railway stations, and it may have come from a station for all I knew. It was simply a flat truck on four wheels, with heavy batteries stored under the platform, and a space in front of the platform for the driver to stand with the controls at waist-level on either side — one side having the Go and Stop button, and the other a horizontal lever to press down or up turning left or right. That was all. Speed about 5 mph at the most, probably less.

It was nevertheless a valuable acquisition. Instead of having to lug the cart down to the town and, particularly, up the hill again, we could now travel by electric conveyance, with me standing on the front as driver, and Jack, or whoever came that day, together with the guard, sitting on the back. I quite enjoyed my little drive each day, bringing the soup or whatever back to the camp, then driving the empty truck over to the works to plug it in to the charger, as a single trip to the town exhausted the batteries and they needed to be charged up all night for the next day. The mere fact of driving this appliance through Zempelburg is associated in my mind with the change that came over Zempelburg at that time.

Christmas — a poor one for us — came and went. The brief flare-up which was to prove to be the last German offensive of the war in the Ardennes also came and went, and the two fronts, east and west, seemed to settle down again. Then suddenly the Eastern front was aflame. On 14 January Marshal Zhukov's armies on the Central Front launched the biggest Soviet offensive of the war on what was virtually the back doorstep of Stalag XXA in Poland. According to the *Beobachter* there were 200 divisions attacking. The mind boggled at this; whether exaggerated or not, the Russian attack was clearly on a scale that would affect us fairly soon. In fact the advance was so swift it was even sooner than we expected.

I was still going down to Zempelburg each day driving my little electric truck, but the town was different now. For two years I had gone down to that small town each day, marching in the roadway if with a party of four or more, or walking the pavement if with a guard alone, or more often lugging the cart for soup or washing. It was a quiet town, which had spent most of the war 1,000 miles from the front on either side. Now it was full of traffic every day, and I was thankful for my electric wagon to weave in and out instead of getting bogged down with the handcart among troops or refugees.

Refugees. We had seen French and Belgians fleeing south away from the German army in 1940; we had seen Germans evacuated to the presumed quiet of the east away from the British firebombing of Bremen and Hamburg in 1943. Now they were Germans again, fleeing west away from the avenging Russians advancing from the east.

They were all the same. Either a dilapidated and overloaded small van, or more often, and indeed almost standard, an open farm cart with one horse and the family sitting on top of the pile of personal belongings on the cart. Always mattresses and bedclothes, always some incongruous item which represented some personal precious possession — a huge picture in an ornate frame, a grandfather clock, a chest of drawers. Quite often there was a dog tied underneath the cart, and I longed to release these dogs, which had to keep trotting as long as the horse kept going, which was most of the day.

There was no enmity to or from these refugees. If I got into a momentary traffic block with them we might exchange a mutual query as to where we had come from, but generally they had no time or emotion left to consider their view of enemy prisoners. They were just humanity caught up in war.

The snow was deep; more snow came and it got deeper. The Russians continued to advance, and one night Moeller called for me to get out the truck and go down the town with a guard to collect the sausage ration. At nine o'clock at night? Something was clearly up.

I got the truck, and managed to get it to the road, which was fairly clear of snow. A guard came out and with him I drove to the town, and to the butcher's. Older people who can remember the war will recall the appearance of a butcher's shop in England; it was the same in Germany only more so. Empty shelves and white tiles that looked as though they had never had meat on them before.

We went in to the back room of the butcher's shop, where he was sitting with his wife and daughter, a plump girl of about 20. They were all very solemn, and although the girl sat quietly and said nothing, I read her face easily enough. She was frightened near to death, and one can hardly blame her. The guard just discussed with the parents the likelihood of our camp moving. I kept quiet and intervened only once, to ask the butcher and his wife why they were wasting time sitting there when they had a daughter with them? Why were they not getting out? They just shrugged. The butcher was one of those people who is incapable of a decision, and I imagine their daughter paid for it later.

We collected some sausage (it was the weekly prisoners' ration, but we never got it — I imagine Meoller had that) and went out again. The traffic and troops had all gone, and the town was dark and silent. The only figure to be seen was a single *Volksturm* (Home Guard), who indicated to me behind the guard's back that he intended to throw his rifle away the moment we had gone. I didn't blame him either.

I managed to get the contraption up the hill again, but with the constant slipping in the snow, this exhausted the batteries completely and I just drove it into the works and left it. It was clear to me that it would be my last trip to Zempelburg.

My deafness has been a nuisance to me all my life, but it does have an occasional bonus, and I got one that night. When I got in to the camp I lay down on my bunk and slept through the night, apparently the only person to do so at Zempelburg on either side of the wire. I was told next morning that the Russians had been firing a barrage through most of the night at some target behind camp, and the whole camp had spent an uncomfortable night. Perhaps I should notch up some sort of score there; there cannot be many men who have slept through a Russian barrage!

Early the following morning we were augmented by the arrival of the prisoners from Schoenhorst, a little farm camp a couple of kilometres along the road, and with them the guards' *Hauptfeldwebel* (Regimental Sergeant-Major). This man had visited the camp from time to time and was the opposite of the accepted picture of an RSM, especially a German RSM. He was quietly spoken, always spoke in a most friendly manner to Seidel or Moeller, and was always courteous to us.

This time he was different. He still did not shout or wave his pistol about, but clearly meant every word he said when he told us we were now to start marching and anyone who dropped out would be shot.

We were all ready to go. That morning German troops, clad in white camouflage hoods and cloaks, had retreated past the camp, crouching in single file. The Russians must have been very close, and since the Germans were showing no signs of decamping and leaving us, we had to march. So we put on all we could manage to wear and packed a bag with whatever we considered essential. There was no soldier's equipment of course — that had been lost in France five years ago — so whatever kit-bag or equivalent we took would have to be carried. We naturally had a better idea of essentials than civilian refugees, but there were still individual personal items which added unnecessary weight, and had to be discarded later.

We assembled in a long line in front of the camp, and right in front of us, less than a mile away across the snow-covered field, there appeared a half-dozen Russian tanks. Astonishingly the tanks stopped, and we turned and marched away without further incident. We might have been liberated there and then by those tanks. Instead we started a march which, in very different conditions, resembled the long march into captivity in 1940. This time, however, our Zempelburg group was only one contingent of a great flow of prisoners evacuated from camps all over Poland and eastern Germany to march away from the advancing Russians. The situation was quite different from the march in 1940. Instead of the hot, dusty roads of France and Belgium in high summer, we stumbled now through knee-deep snow in sub-zero temperatures, and we were to sleep in barns or even in the snow in this cold. We were without food, and were to remain without food for most of the march, as well as having started after a long period of short commons with no Red Cross parcels to augment our watery soup.

Much later, as these columns were liberated and their stories were heard, the Allied press coined a phrase for this march. They called it the Death March.

9

The Murder Roster

We knew this would be no picnic. The snow was a foot deep, and we had been living at barely subsistence level since the drying-up of Red Cross parcels months earlier, but at the start of the second great march even the most pessimistic could not have foreseen the trials that lay ahead. The blizzard, the intense cold, sapping even the will to live, the frostbites, the weeks on end with no food issue when we would be glad to gnaw on raw swedes dug out with our bare hands from the iron-hard frozen ground, and, above all, the long wandering march, when, like so many earthbound Flying Dutchmen, we would plod more than 800 miles in a long haul that started in the depth of a Polish winter and ended in a German spring. For me personally there was to be the incident of the murder roster, and on a more pleasant occasion, my unexpected opportunity to assist an American general, an assistance repaid handsomely later on. But all this lay ahead as we trudged through the thick snow and glanced back at Zempelburg camp for the last time.

Notwithstanding the conditions there was no pessimism at the start; nor, except perhaps on the second day, throughout the whole affair. The war might yet last another six months or even longer, but Germany was clearly desperately on the defensive, and surely a final Allied victory could not be longer delayed than the present year. All we had to do was to stay alive. So we marched. Some didn't make it.

It was hard going through the snow, but there was one aspect that gave great satisfaction. Unlike the march in 1940 (always referred to as The March, as though the present one didn't count quite so much), when the guards in France either had motor transport or at least bicycles, this time the guards had to march with us. We were in no hurry, and in fact tried several times to slow the pace in the hope that the Russians would catch us up; but the guards had no desire to see the Red Army, and urged the column on with the one unanswerable argument available to them, the rifle. Real speed was impossible in those conditions, but we kept up a reasonable pace as we left Zempelburg behind us.

We had not gone far when we came across a man struggling to push a car that was stuck in the snow. It was Pollvogts, the *Betriebsmeister*, and he was glad to see us and to ask the guards for prisoners' help in pushing it. The guards made a few men give a half-hearted push, but the car only moved a few feet in the snow and the guards were not going to waste time on a civilian with the Russian army behind them. They told the prisoners to leave him and get on, so the former lord and master of the Zempelburg sawmills was left behind.

We plodded on ... and on ... and on. At one point we were beginning to succeed in slowing the pace when we passed a field with a battery of German guns in it. We were halfway past them when they opened fire at some unseen target. We knew quite enough about the likely response of the Russian artillery, and the pace perceptibly quickened until we were past the battery and into the woods.

When we stopped very late at night the general consensus of opinion was that we had covered 30 miles that day, all through deep snow. We were herded into a barn, where we climbed onto the hay, removed only our boots, and slept the sleep of the exhausted.

I was awakened by a combination of shouting and banging, accompanied by acute discomfort. It was a wonder I had slept at all: I must have been very tired indeed. The straw had shifted with my body movements during the night and I was almost vertical. I struggled out of the straw, my mind returning to consciousness with speedy identification of the shouts, which were from the guards: *'Raus! Raus!'* We were to get very used to a night in a barn and an awakening to *'Raus! Raus!'*

The banging took a few seconds longer to trace. It was all round me, and insistent. I looked round. Everywhere the prisoners were sitting up on the straw banging their boots together. Why on earth should they do that? Had they all gone off their heads at the same time?

The guards were urgently screaming their *Raus*; for some reason they wanted to get us on the road without delay, and some were prodding the straw with their bayonets to make sure there was no one hiding or dilatory in getting up. My boots. Where were my boots? I felt panic rising as men were being roused out of the straw clutching their boots, but still without them on their feet. If I got out into the road without boots my feet would be frostbitten very quickly. I delved into the straw, helped by Phin who had slept at my side, and eventually located the boots well buried in the straw. Then I understood the banging.

The temperature in the barn may have been fractionally

higher than outside, but it was still sub-zero, and my boots, like all the others, were frozen solid, even though they had been buried in the straw. It was quite impossible to put them on in this state and I hobbled out of the barn in my socks, banging my boots together like the rest to try to induce at least a little suppleness sufficient to pull them onto my feet.

Somehow we all managed it, but after that the boots stayed on the feet at night. The barn was on the outskirts of a small village, and as we cleared the village out into the open country we found we were not alone, and were mixed up with at least two other columns of prisoners. Some were Russian, some British. The Russians did not affect us — we would easily have separated ourselves later on — but the recognition of the British prisoners was more serious. Most of us knew at least a few friends in *Stalag*, and this was clearly the main stream of prisoners from the headquarters camp at *Stalag*. This meant a lot more guards, perhaps officers, perhaps even Makensen.

Hauptmann Makensen was in charge at *Stalag*, and a very ugly customer indeed. No matter what lay ahead of us, it would surely be worse if we were under Makensen's authority. We wanted no part of *Stalag*, especially that officer. And there he was stalking up and down the column telling the guards to press us on.

The *Stalag* column had obviously been on the road some days, and many looked as if they were staggering along at the end of their tether. We passed one prisoner, whom I recognised as a headquarters *Stalag* worker and a member of my own regiment, sitting in the snow by the roadside surrounded by a couple of large bags and some bits and pieces of tins and eating utensils, just repeating to no one in particular that he could go no further and they could shoot him there. No one stopped to help him and

I do not know what became of him. Judging from the stuff round him he was carrying too much, and would have done better to get rid of most of it.

The Zempelburg lot had already done that. We knew we were in for a march in the snow and had brought away only what we thought were essentials in the first place; but already, half-way through the first day, most of us had ruthlessly delved into the kitbag or whatever else we had packed our gear in and thrown a great deal of it away — even, I had noticed, handkerchiefs. Anything to lighten the load.

It was very cold. Most of us had no gloves and had wrapped our hands with rags, or more usually, socks. Underneath our army caps some had a variety of real or makeshift balaclavas, but most only had the army cap pulled down as far as it would go. The cold wind grew stronger, and suddenly the whole column vanished. Russians, British, German guards, all vanished. Instead the air was full of driving snow — not gentle snowflakes, but tiny particles that stung the face like needles, driven almost horizontally by a fierce wind.

In five years in Poland, none of us had ever experienced the like of this blizzard. There could have been 500, 1,000 or 10,000 men in that column, but nothing could be seen beyond the nearest man, and that only providing he was not more than a few feet away. Phin and I somehow stuck together. Figures loomed up and vanished again as we staggered on. No one had any idea of direction except to go forward and hope it would lead somewhere, sometime, to some shelter from this unrelenting, killing wind and snow.

There was no question of any form of speech in the scream of the blizzard, but it was as well we had kept together. Every now and then I would point with my balled fist, clutching on to my rags of socks, to Phin's nose, where the tip had started to go intense white. He would rub it vigourously and point to my ear lobes, which were showing the same symptoms. Frostbite we could do without.

A figure appeared beside me staggering worse than I. It was a Russian, and he made the universal sign asking for food. I shook my head and stumbled on. He persisted, making the sign again. I had a piece of bread in my battledress pocket, but it was not only all I had, it would have been quite impossible to pause to delve into a pocket with my sock-gloved hand in that howling wind. I shook my head again and he just dropped flat. He could not possibly have survived, and I felt I had just killed someone.

We seemed to be on an endless plain. There was no food, no hedges, no trees, no shelter, just snow and that merciless, screaming banshee wind. If a sock or hand-rag flapped loose, if a coat loosened from a button, there was no possibility of putting it together, no respite for anything from that wind.

It went on for hours. There was no sense of time, just the agonising misery of total cold and the unrelenting blizzard, driving a million particles of ice into the face or any unprotected portion of skin. Once we thought we heard shots fairly close, but it was difficult to be sure of anything in the howl of the storm.

Eventually, at what proved to be early evening, the storm abated sufficiently to see part of the plain ahead. There were figures over a wide area, most stumbling, and some almost on their knees, with guards making some effort to close up the column. There were only British prisoners, and it transpired that the Russians we had seen were from a column ahead of the *Stalag* party and some of them had fallen behind, where they either caught up if they could, or were shot, or simply expired. Our own case seemed bad enough to us, but we were all well

165

aware of the food situation of the Russians during the whole of their captivity. There were no Red Cross parcels for them, and most of them had started their captivity in the prison camps in a weak state, after whatever marches or treatment they may have had from the point of capture.

Not that we gave much thought to Russians or anyone else at the end of that terrible day. The wind had dropped a little, but the cold was still there, the snow was still there, the guards were still there urging us on, and all we could do was stumble on until the advent of shelter or collapse, whichever came first.

Ahead men were bobbing up and down as if they were jumping. They were in fact doing exactly that. There was a snow-covered gully of some sort in the way, and Mackensen was on the far side of it, brandishing his revolver and screaming to men to get over and keep moving. So as we got to the gully we jumped; it was not very much of an obstacle, probably just a wide and deep ditch, and somehow it seemed to mark the end of that awful day.

Once we had passed Mackensen we found ourselves back on a road which passed a farm, and Moeller was there, syphoning the Zempelburg group into the farm area, leaving the much larger *Stalag* party to stagger on past it with their guards.

The farm was deserted, and there was no question of food, but it did at least offer shelter. The farmhouse was kept for Moeller and the guards, but the prisoners were allowed to find whatever shelter they could for the night in the other buildings. I cannot remember what comfort Phin and I found for ourselves that night; I can only remember the two men who had been first in the farm and had crawled into the pigsty to lay claim to it as their own for the night.

Our gentlemanly *Hauptfeldwebel* vanished, presumably picked up by Mackensen to join the larger *Stalag* column, and

Moeller was left in charge. This undoubtedly was the reason for the stop in the farm. Neither Moeller nor his guards would have any great wish to get tied up with the main *Stalag* party and come under Hauptmann Mackensen's command.

Nor did we. The following morning we started off. Again we marched some 20 miles, and again we put up in a farm for the night, this time in a barn, as on the first night. This became a pattern; a long march by day through the snow and a sojourn in a barn at night. The advantage of a barn from the guards' point of view is obvious; all they had to do was make sure they got all the prisoners inside, and they could then mount a small and easy guard on the door.

There was no food issued in this early period, and we grubbed what we could out of the ground. As the ground was snow-covered and rock-hard, and we had to keep moving all the time anyway, our prospects of getting anything were remote in the first place, but we did manage to get some swedes occasionally. To be fair, Moeller and Loeschner, his *Obergefreiter* and clerk, tried to get us some bread; but with other prisoner columns on the move, as well as the obvious priority for the guards, we did not do very well during this early time. Come to that, we did not do very well for official issues most of the time, but it was worse in the first ten days, during which, to the best of my memory, we had no food issue at all.

We occasionally met other columns, but *Kommandants* of other groups kept their prisoners and guards separate from ours, just as Moeller was doing in our own case, and we always drifted away again. We did however pick up odds and ends now and again, so that our column, which had started from Zempelburg 100 strong, numbered somewhere around 300 by the time of my escape at the end of March. During the whole of this time we had different British commanders but I remained *Dolmetscher*, and since I negotiated for food, had virtual responsibility for the column until I left it. Notwithstanding my total lack of rank, this was accepted by both sides, guards and prisoners, and the result in the way of Red Cross will be seen in due course.

We had been marching for eight days, and already numbered around 200 when we stopped overnight in an abandoned brickworks instead of the usual barn. Here I experienced one of the most bizarre, as well as one of the most chilling, episodes.

* * *

As we filtered into the brickworks we were in our usual state of exhaustion, cold and hungry. The brickworks covered a large area of ground, and the building into which we were herded by the guards was itself very large and high. It was almost totally dark inside, and the guards, having no single door to guard, wandered among us the whole time. It was of course bitterly cold, and some of the chaps, who had managed to dig up some potatoes during the day, scrounged bits of wood and lit fires to roast their spuds. This meant that very shortly after we entered the building there were groups of prisoners standing around smoky little fires, with the smoke curling up to the high roof. Since there was more smoke than fire from the snow-damp wood, the inside of the brickworks where the prisoners were gathered had the dim appearance of a pre-war London fog, with the mere outlines of men standing round some small glow here and there, the smoke rising, and the occasional shape of a figure with a rifle.

Suddenly someone approached me and spoke in French. He turned out to be a Yugoslav officer, who was nothing to do with us; he had spoken to one of the chaps in French and been directed to me to deal with.

The use of French was very unusual among prisoners; German, the language of our captors, was the normal means of communication between nationalities of differing speech. Still there it was, and his French was a great deal better than mine. With a bit of my French and a bit of his German here and there, he told his story.

He had been with a group of Polish and Serbian officer prisoners who, like ourselves, had passed this way a few days ago and had been shacked up in the brickworks for the night. He and one of the Polish officers had escaped from the group during the night and hidden in the brickworks when the column marched on in the morning. This would not have been too difficult once they got away from the main group, as although the morning count would have revealed the discrepancy there was never time for more than a quick search before moving on.

Indeed, in our own case we had sometimes been roused out in the night to move on, without any counting at all, but only a quick bayonet stabbing search of the straw in the barn before starting the march.

He and his friend had hidden in the brickworks on the night of their escape, and on the following day had decided to stay hidden until the area was overrun by the Russians, as it certainly would be in due course. This was the very purpose of moving the prisoners. However, they had soon found they were not alone. Others had escaped from other columns which had also used the brickworks for the night, and there was apparently a group of escapers hidden up somewhere in the building.

They would obviously not normally contact other prisoner columns to seek recruits, it would be too dangerous, but in our case we had special merit. They had observed our arrival and realised we were British. This was something they had been waiting for. They wanted one or more British prisoners to join them, for a reason which was easy for me to understand then but might seem to a reader at the least somewhat tenuous today.

The escapers, of whom I knew no more thus far than I have recounted, were all from the Eastern European states. It must be remembered that these were the days of the Big Three, when not only was Britain on an equal footing in the war with the USA and the USSR, but in the eyes of most of Europe, the British Prime Minister was the real leader of the West. The brickworks fugitives, having escaped from German captivity, did not want to find that when the Russians arrived they had merely exchanged one captivity for another. The object of the escape was to get back to their own country. Since Russia was one of the Allied Big Three, it could be presumed that any British or American prisoners of war who were liberated by the Red Army would be sent back to their own country. If, therefore, this escape group, whoever they were, could get a couple of British or American soldiers to join them, surely this would mean that when the Russians arrived all the members of this group would be sent back to their own country on the grounds that the British or American members of the group would automatically go back home, and anyone with them would go home as well.

To the modern reader this must sound like grasping at a small straw, but that is exactly what one does in a war.

Well, there it was. Could I find any of the comrades willing to escape and join them? I told him this was no problem at all. I was not prepared to go alone, but if my friend would come with me he need look no further.

I am not at all sure how the matter would have fared if I had passed the word round generally. Despite the harsh conditions of our march, we had already endlessly compared this march with the first one in 1940, and were all agreed this was the better bet. This time we were marching in the right direction, to the west; it would surely not be long before the Western Allies made their heave and thrust into Germany, and the majority held the view that there was no point in unnecessary risks at this stage, especially to turn east. I am bound to say I would have had the same view in the normal way, but this was offered on a plate. These people evidently already had a hidey-hole available, and the very pressure of our march indicated the Russians could not be too far away.

Les Alsop was immediately ready to come, and I told the Yugoslav officer two of us were available.

All would have been well (or at least, different) if this new contact had not been so anxious to please. This group of escapers somewhere in the brickworks had been awaiting the arrival of either a British or American column to achieve their desired addition, and this gentleman had been sent to recruit one or two. He now had two, Les and myself, but instead of inviting us to get moving, he said he would first take me on my own to show me how well they were organised and what a good hiding-place they had. I could then come back and collect my friend. Since this meant I must first get away without observation by the guards, then come back and do it all over again, this was an unnecessary double jeopardy. But he insisted, and in one way it was not a bad thing for us, as it would leave Les time to make preparation from our kit to take whatever we might feel we ought to hang on to.

Although this was an escape, it was really too easy to rank with the great escapes recorded by others. The fact that this officer, in a different uniform from the rest of us, had joined our group and stood chatting with me for some time, indicates how dark it was in the brickworks; the guards were themselves shadowy figures moving among shadowy groups of prisoners.

There was no difficulty at all in choosing an appropriate moment and slipping away from the rest, and in short order we were in almost total darkness, and of course bitter cold, moving along passageways and piles of bricks.

We came to the end of a passage with a couple of steps up and a door, on which my guide knocked with some special knock. The door was opened in darkness, but clearly the light had only been switched off to open the door, as it was switched on again as soon as the door was closed.

I was now in a well-lit room, not unlike a prison camp room, without any tables or chairs, but with a couple of up-and-down wooden bunks against the wall. It seemed that most of them slept on the floor, as there were at least a dozen in the room, perhaps one or two more than that. I noticed a man in Polish officer's uniform, presumably the companion of my guide, a couple or other men in civilian clothes, and eight or ten women. Two or three of the women had dresses, but most were clad in the blue and white striped garments of the concentration camps; they were emaciated, and several had sores of the type seen on our own prisoners in the early days, the result of malnutrition. I had no time to get any more than these general impressions as the leader came forward immediately and the subsequent talk required my whole attention during the time I was in the room.

The leader was one of the women in civilian dress, and there was no doubt about her authority. During the time she was talking to me the rest of the room were moving about their own business, apparently taking no notice of us, but no one else attempted to join the conversation and I could almost feel her command over both women and men, and officers at that. She was in command of herself as well, clean and without sores, decisive in speech, and, I soon found, utterly ruthless.

I judged her age to be somewhere around mid-thirties, or perhaps a little older. The only reason I thought about age, or remember it now, is because at one point in conversation- - fairly one-sided, as she did the talking — she threw out a casual invitation to sleep with her if my friend and I decided to join the group. Despite my long celibacy I was not too keen, as she seemed so old. I was young in more ways than one in those days, and if the memory brings a wry mental smile in my more mature years, there was nothing else humorous in the episode.

She explained what they were all doing there, and why they would like to have either British or American escapers with them. She offered neither favour nor entreaty. We could come or not as we pleased, and if we came we must accept the risk with the rest of them. I felt privileged and pleased that there was no mention of the risk they had already taken in making contact with the new bunch of prisoners; she was giving me a trust, which, if betrayed, would mean their deaths, but she never mentioned it.

It seemed that the women were there first, having escaped some 12 days earlier when a large column of prisoners from a concentration camp had passed through the brickworks one night. They were Baltic Jewesses, from Estonia, Latvia and Lithuania, and had been in German camps since the early days of the Russo-German war. It was not difficult to envisage who took the quick decision to organise and lead that particular escape. They found this room and hid up, and when they were later joined by other escapers, found wood and built a couple of bunks, fixed the electric light, and organised a mode of living which had the simple object of staying alive. I knew about the two officers, but never found out where the other two or three men came from. Nor did I learn the name of the leader, although I am sure that if I had stayed to read the roster I would have found her name at the top.

During the conversation, as she was explaining the situation, she pointed to a piece of paper stuck to the door with some names on it — say five or six, not enough for the whole room — and said that as my friend and I were soldiers we would no doubt wish our names to be added. This was put in the same manner as the offer to join them, take it or leave it, but I gathered we would be expected to take part in whatever activity was represented by this list. It looked a common enough item, the sort of thing that might be pinned to any barrack-room door as a fatigue roster, to make sure everyone takes his turn and does his bit. *But this was a murder roster.*

Every two or three days, as it got towards evening — still early enough for people to be moving about but already quite dark — a couple of the group would go into the local town (I never knew which town, they came and went on the march), find some civilian on his, or preferably her, own, knife them, take their top clothes, ration cards and money, and the next day one of the women could go down to the town and get rations. This is how they were living.

I dare say I was a little taken back, but not especially startled. We were living through times and conditions where abnormality was normal every day; I was after all standing in a secret room among desperate men and women, chatting as if at a tea-party. My new lady friend was simply telling me of a situation and I was simply listening to it.

But I knew I would not be able to do it. I knew I did not have whatever it takes to commit deliberate murder even in those conditions and to an enemy in time of war, nor did I even have the courage to express clear refusal. I did not have to. She could sense it, and I dare say England's name sunk a little in her eyes with a supposed soldier so chicken-hearted. (The reader who feels that this account seems too cold-blooded to be true should reflect on the inhuman conditions under which these people, particularly the women, had been living for years. If their own lives were of no account to their captors, why should they be squeamish themselves? They were probably all nice young ladies before the war.)

She became very businesslike. Here then, was the situation; if I now changed my mind it would be understood. If I and my friend still wanted to come we would be welcome. The fact that we were British was of some importance to them for reasons already explained, and on that account it would be a matter for us if we wished to go on the roster or not. All understood? Good. Then I could return to the others, pick up my friend and get away to join the group. She told me, smiling, to be careful not to get caught getting away, but had no doubt we could deal with that easily enough. My initial guide would take me back to somewhere near the British group, and then leave me on my own. When my friend and I got away we should not try to find the room, but simply find somewhere to hide up till daylight, when they would find us and, as it were, take us into their bosom.

My guide took me back as arranged to the outskirts of the Zempelburg group and left me. The picture was the same as when I left — still the smoky fires with the little groups of vague figures huddled round them, still the same odd guard appearing, too cold himself to do more than take a token stroll around. All was as if I had only shut my eyes for a few seconds and then opened them again. Yet I had been away two hours, standing in a fully lighted room among a gang of cut-throats, chatting with a murderess. But a woman of fibre, a true leader. Would I share her bunk, or would the offer be withdrawn if I didn't go on the roster?

I didn't go back. Although I do not hesitate to acknowledge my own cowardice in so many fields, that was not the reason for my failure to return in this case. Indeed, as I got back to the prisoners, I was looking forward to introducing Les to the leader (I never knew her name) as if I were already an old friend of hers. Nor would there have been any difficulty in getting away, nor in finding some hidey-hole in this huge brick complex until the column moved on the next day.

Perhaps there is after all some fate that guides our destiny. As I am not a philosopher I wouldn't know, but fate had certainly effected an odd trick during my brief absence. When I got back to Les he was flat on his back and in pain. He had been all right when I left him but, just as had happened to me once at Rittel in the early days, his knee had swollen up like a balloon. He was quite immobile, and would have to go on the sick-cart the next day. (The guards had acquired a horse and cart somewhere along the way, and this was used for the guards' baggage and the sick. The sick in this context meant total incapacity to stand up; for anything less you marched.)

So next morning I saw Moeller and Les was admitted to the sick-cart, while Phin and I marched off with the others. I was not of the mettle of Jim O'Donnell and would not have gone on my own, but I would have liked to have given the lady an explanation. I wonder if they made it? I hope so, although my failure to return with my friend as arranged probably caused England's name to sink a little further.

* * *

On the road once more in the snow, Moeller and the guards were becoming more experienced in the affair now, and we began to get food. Loeschner or one of the guards would go ahead to see what could be arranged in the next village in the way of bread or potatoes, and to seek some appropriate barn or similar accommodation for the night for the prisoners as well as billets for the guards. Loeschner has not appeared in these pages until this winter march, but he was the *Schreiber*, or clerk, at Zempelburg from Seidel's time and was very efficient. He was a serious person, and used to discuss the war with me, always on the assumption that Hitler would somehow produce some unexpected weapon that would result in Germany winning the war. He could not understand the British light-hearted attitude to war and almost everything else. For him this attitude was epitomised in the British habit of wearing the cap on one side of the head instead of centrally on the top. We once made a replica of a British tin helmet for a play, and Loeschner got me to put it on. Without even thinking about it, I had put it on tilted to one side.

'There,' said Loeschner, 'look how sporty that looks, not serious for war at all!'

He then got me to put his own German helmet on, and told me to look in the mirror and see how much more serious I looked, much more the stern soldier type. I had to admit he was right, but pointed out that Tommies wore their battle bowlers that way in the last war also, and won it. Loeschner still thought we did not regard war earnestly enough.

Once we started getting bread, an ominously increasing number of men looked for a fire or stove to toast their bread until it was black. Burnt bread was the accepted antidote for dysentery, and most of us had at least a passing bout of it at some time in the march. For some it persisted, and with the constant cold and marching, brought for many an era of continuing weakness and misery, with the ever-present companion of possible final collapse.

Then we came to Hammerstein. Unexpected, incredible, wonderful Hammerstein.

There was nothing wonderful about it when we arrived. It was in abandoned prison camp which we entered for the night. It had been last used by Russians, the huts were abominably filthy, with excreta everywhere, in and out of the huts, and the whole place stank to high heaven. Some chaps went into the huts and immediately came out again, preferring to sleep in the snow rather than in such shelter. Phin and I found a place that was not too bad; neither of us had any intention of sleeping in the snow if we could help it.

The following morning, as we prepared to take the snow-bound road again the wonder of Hammerstein was revealed. One of the huts was not filthy, not smelly. It was the store, and packed to the roof with British Red Cross parcels!

We would not be allowed to stay, we must move on, but clearly this bonanza could not be left behind. Needs must when the Devil drives. With no tools but our hands, boards were wrenched out of the huts and smashed into smaller pieces, nails pushed out, straightened, and driven in again, string found or cloth torn and strung together for rope, and as we assembled to march out every pair of muckers was towing a home-made sledge piled with four or five Red Cross parcels.

Now the snow was our friend. We could not possibly carry these parcels, and the going was of course harder dragging our makeshift sledges, but without that transport we would not be able to carry many of the tins. It was getting a little warmer, but still sub-zero, and each morning we looked anxiously for signs that the ice was still there and the thaw had not yet started.

With the conditions of the march, the contents of the parcels could not be spun out in the way we had been used to in a regular prison camp; but they were a godsend and kept us going for two or three weeks.

The snow did not last long. One morning we saw water dripping from the roofs of houses, and realised the thaw had come at last. At the end of that day there was an abandoned orgy of eating, and we packed our kit and pockets with whatever we felt we could carry.

It was on the day of the thaw, with snow still fairly thick on the ground, that I got some view of what it must have been like for refugees to leave their homes in a hurry and take to the road. We had stopped for a momentary rest near a house in an otherwise empty landscape; the door was open, it was clear no one was inside, but a few of us went into the house. The guards did not stop us, but one of them came in and told us not to break any furniture as no doubt the inhabitants would be coming back when the war was over.

The place had been left in such a hurry that there was a large pot of stew on the stove still warm, and we doled it out and ate it. I can remember that stew now as being too salty. I felt for the family that had lived a normal and civilised life in their own home, and then abandoned it in such a hurry as to leave the door open for strangers — who would almost certainly be soldiers and probably enemies — to come in and trample all over the place, eating their stew and looting their possessions. In fact we did not do any looting there, but that would certainly have been the eventual fate of that house, like so many others throughout

Europe in the changing fortunes of six years of total war.

On and ever on each day, now in this direction, now that. It was no use asking the guards where we were going. I had no doubt Moeller was telling me the truth when he said he didn't know from one day to the next. There was some contact with his company commander, presumably Mackensen, as orders appeared to come through from somewhere for the next destination, but the fact was quite plain that Moeller didn't care anymore. In fact he said so to me more than once.

We came to Swinemunde (Polish Swincojscie); I have since checked this on a map and reckon we had already marched at least twice the crow-fly distance from Sepolno to get there. Here we crossed the harbour in a ferry; it was still very cold, and the harbour was full of floating ice. On the far side was a small group of Italian soldiers, some of the very small number who had elected to stay in the war on the Fascist side after the Badoglio surrender in 1943. They were nominally Mussolini's soldiers, but of course, like Mussolini himself, under German orders. They were a very sorry looking bunch, and on the docks at Swinemunde, with ice around them, the Russians approaching, and no one, not even the Germans, interested in them, their future was pretty bleak. They must have wished they had stayed in sunny Italy.

Then on further, through Mecklenburg. The Red Cross windfall from Hammerstein was gone by now, but as both guards and prisoners became more accustomed to this strange nomadic way of life, it was not always Loeschner who went ahead on his own. The Red Cross parcels stored at Hammerstein had made us realise that there must be other camps in Germany with such stores, and I would sometimes go ahead with Loeschner to seek information as to whether any such parcels could be obtained.

On one of these occasions word was heard that there was

a Red Cross parcel dump at a certain town some few miles off our route. After consultation with Moeller, Loeschner and I took one of the carts. (Our first cart-horse had collapsed and died from exhaustion after constant whipping one night to haul too great a load through too-deep snow at too fast a pace; one of the guards had gone to a farm to commandeer a new horse, and had obtained a second horse and cart as well.)

We got to a town, name long forgotten, where we found the German *Kommandantur*, which seemed the most likely place to enquire after Red Cross parcels. There, Loeschner left me in some sort of waiting room while he went to make enquiries. There were already two soldiers in this room, the first American uniforms I had ever seen. One of them was a young man of my own age or probably younger, and quite smartly dressed. The other was an older man who looked more like our own chaps, in the sense of being somewhat unkempt and having clearly slept in his clothes for some time. I took no notice of the older man, and chatted to the younger. I had noticed the older man had eagles on his epaulettes, but this meant nothing to me. I knew the eagle was the American emblem, as it was the German, and German soldiers had the eagle on their uniform, so presumably the Yanks did also. In fact the insignia was that of a full colonel, who in this case was a brevet Brigadier General. (This is strictly an American title. The rank of Brigadier-General was abolished in the British army after the First World War and replaced by the present rank of Brigadier.) I saw the chap looking for some sign of rank on my uniform and told him I was just a private, but that I was the interpreter of our column, and on that account had come here to try and get our lot some Red Cross. At this the older man leaned over and said he had a similar column, and also wanted to get some food. Could I help him as well by interpretation? I said I would be glad to, and it was somewhere around here that the younger man addressed the older as 'General' and I was put in the picture.

The General was the senior officer from a column of American officers who had started marching a week ago and had so far had very little food, so on his insistence one of their guards had brought him here to argue the toss with the local senior German officer. I do not remember enquiring or being told what the private was doing there; presumably they had some batmen among their number.

In due course both Loeschner and the General's own guard appeared, and the General and I were admitted to an office where there was a German major. There was no waste of time; the major knew what we had come for and said there was a Red Cross store quite near, as there had been a prison camp somewhere nearby until it was evacuated. We could therefore have enough Red Cross parcels for our group — he gave me the number which was correct and had presumably been given him by Loeschner, who would have reported accurately when anyone else would have bumped the number up. However he, the major, could not authorise the issue of such parcels to the Americans as they were British parcels — unless of course I was prepared to say we had no objection. I said of course we had no objection, and the matter was settled.

Outside, the General and his private were taken off by their guard, presumably back to their column or to get transport for the parcels. This General had spoken to me, not like a high-ranking officer to a private, but more as an equal, and parted from me with the thanks of a friend. I was, however, to see him again.

Loeschner and I went to the Red Cross store, loaded our wagon with the appropriate number of parcels, and jogged off to the village which was to be the rendezvous for the end of that day's march.

The delight on our arrival can be imagined, and I was especially touched when the parcels were handed out. There was one over, not through any deliberation, simply through some miscounting in loading, and the whole column called out for me to keep it. Which I did.

Then onwards. The Red Cross gave out and we were again out of food. Spirits were excellent, as by this time we knew the Western Allies had crossed the Rhine and were advancing into Germany. But for many health was very low, and dysentery was rife.

One night we stopped in a barn which had a tiled roof, constructed in such a manner that each row of tiles was separated from the next with several inches of daylight in between. As we settled in, I felt barns were cold enough without this addition of fresh air. Odd how one remembers small details like that to associate with greater incidents — in this case a fatality.

If there was one man as well known on the column as I, it was Spud Taylor, our medical orderly. He had no medicine, but had never ceased to do his best. On one occasion I had managed to get him to a German medical officer in some town, but it had not proved possible to get any supplies. Spud asked him if there was anything at all that could be obtained to deal with the dysentery, and the MO said all that was required was raw potatoes; squeeze the potato and drink the resultant liquid. This was new to Spud, and new to me also. We tried it, but I cannot say whether it was effective, and whether the gradual recoveries were due to nature or were assisted by this simple remedy. Most men placed their faith in burnt toast.

On the night of the ventilated barn, I got settled in and then went in search of Spud. The guards of course knew me well, and were used to me going in and out. I just asked a guard at the barn door if he knew where the Sani was, and he directed me to a house, where I found Spud in a bare downstairs room.

There were three men in the room: Spud, another chap assisting him, and a third man prone and motionless on his stomach on the floor. Spud was glad to see me, as he and his companion had been taking turns to administer artificial respiration and were exhausted. He showed me what to do and I took over. I had only been at it for about 20 minutes when I felt exhausted too, but the other two had been at it for the better part of two hours. From then on we took it in turns until the early hours of the morning, until Spud wearily acknowledged it was no use. The man had been dead for some time.

The following morning Moeller sent the two of us with a *Gefreiter* on the cart to take the body away. I did not know this *Gefreiter*. We had picked up a few new guards on the way as well as extra prisoners.

He took the cart to the outskirts of some town and told us to leave the body there. The place was clearly a rubbish damp and we protested strongly, but he was adamant that it was only temporary and someone else would come and give the man a decent burial. This was nonsense, but there was nothing we could do about it: the fellow obviously had orders to get rid of the body and catch up the column, which was already on the move again.

We placed the man — one of the additions I didn't know — carefully on the ground, and the guard called out to us to stop wasting time and just throw the body on the dump. I remember him calling out, 'He can't feel it!'

There was no doubt about the cause of death, whatever may have been the technical term a normal doctor would have put on the death certificate. The chap had been in the final stages of exhaustion, malnutrition and amoebic dysentery. He was not the only one, but others managed to carry on, and we were lucky that was the only death on this column — there were more on the larger ones.

Still onwards. We only marched through one large town, that of Celle. It was untouched by war, and I read after the war that the RAF had 121 towns in Germany on their bombing list and had bombed 120 of them. Celle was the lucky exception.

Near Celle we had our only ride; we entrained in the usual cattle trucks for we knew not where. The journey was not very long and stopped somewhere near a large town, which proved to be Hildesheim.

Hildesheim had been heavily bombed, and next to the railway was the gutted shell of what had apparently been a large sugar factory, as the sugar had run down onto the railway lines and hardened into toffee. We broke this off the lines and ate it, spitting out the pieces of railway-track ballast stuck on it.

We did not go through the town, but stopped in the usual barn outside. Les Alsop was mucking in with Phin and I by this time, and although it was now spring it was still cold and the three of us huddled together in the straw for warmth.

We marched on, still hungry, when rumour came that there was some Red Cross in a town not far off our march. I went there with one of the guards and a cart, and in the town saw some Americans in a little chain, passing Red Cross parcels to a cart of their own. We could see these were American Red Cross parcels. Would we be able to get them?

As I got down from the cart one of the soldiers in the chain called out to me: it was the General whom I had met in a previous town, just one in a chain like the privates. He called out to our guard that it was all OK, and called to me to take what we wanted.

So we did. We loaded our cart with American Red Cross parcels. The General called to me not to take the British parcels — there were both in this store — but to take the American ones as they had cigarettes in them. (We had also received cigarettes with our own Red Cross parcels, but parcels and cigarettes were separate; in the American system they were all in one parcel, and their food was rather better, with always a quarter-pound of coffee, whereas ours had two ounces of tea.)

My General friend called out some pleasantries to me as if to an old friend, but there was no time for chit-chat. He did not stop in his chain; either he had a large column or was stocking up well.

This proved to be our last issue of Red Cross, and almost the end of the march for me.

We marched on, now here, now there, and although we had long since lost much sense of direction it was clear now we had turned about and were now marching east. The Allies were now closer than the Russians.

Les Alsop had recovered from his swollen knee, and we decided we would seek some chance to get away and try to get to the Americans who were reported to be only about 30 miles away.

Not long after leaving Hildesheim we were billeted one night in the usual barn just outside a little village called Sirium. Moeller arranged for the farmer to supply some potatoes, and a few men were allowed out of the barn to a small outhouse where they boiled the spuds in the boiler normally used for boiling the potato peelings for the pigs. It was already dark, and the spud-boiling party was moving in and around their outhouse, frequently out of sight of the guard on the barn. I consulted with Les. This would be it. It was up to me to devise some means of getting us both to the spud-boiling party, and then slipping away from it. After that we would rely on a combination of luck and our wits to avoid recapture and gain our final freedom.

10

The Last Escape

Since my role of Dolmetscher made it easier for me to get out of the barn than the others, we decided to approach this on the lines of a little reconnaissance first by myself; if this revealed some unexpected obstacle, such as guards in the wrong place, nothing would be lost, and if some particular path was discovered that might prove easier something would be gained.

There was no difficulty in getting out; I just nodded to the door guard and told him I was going over to the outhouse to see how the potato boiling was getting on. He nodded back, and suffered me to proceed. The outhouse was in any case in his full view all the time and he probably didn't give it a second thought.

Outside the shed door, however, I glanced back at the guard, who had already turned his back on me to watch the barn door, and ran up a flight of stone steps adjacent to the shed leading into a three-storied house.

On the large state farms in Germany it was fairly easy to see which of the farm buildings was the actual farmhouse, and as this obviously was not, it was an even bet that it housed some French or Polish forced labourers. Inside the door I was faced with a bare passage with doors on each side. I chose the nearest one on the left and went in.

The first glance reassured me that the occupants were not Germans. The sole furniture of the room consisted of a deal table with a few broken-down chairs and a small iron stove, on which a slovenly looking girl was cooking what was by this time the national dish in Germany — potatoes. Other ill-dressed girls and a couple of youths sat or stood about the room.

My entry was greeted with a mixture of fear and anxiety to assist. I was asked in extremely bad German whether the guard had seen me come in and, on my assurance that he had not, they plied me with cold boiled potatoes and a slice of bread. I had assumed on seeing them that they were Poles, but it transpired otherwise. They were Italians, brought from Italy after the surrender and forced to work for the Germans. The people occupying the rooms on the other side of the passage were Ukrainians. All were half-starved and longing for the Americans to come and liberate them.

Although they had been in Germany 18 months, none of them seemed able to speak German at all, and I struggled to wrench my mind back to the elementary Italian I had learnt from that German primer back in the Schlüsselmühle days. Eventually I managed to get them to understand that I wanted them to hide a friend and myself for the night. Friendly though they were, this they would not do, for they lived in mortal fear of the Gestapo — who, it appeared, had made several visits in the middle of the night.

Finally, they agreed to show me how I could get into the attic, although they were not to see me get up there and I must be away before midnight. I agreed to this perforce and, having dodged down the stone steps back to the shed, strolled back to the barn to collect my friend.

That night there was fine drizzle falling, which, although a trifle uncomfortable, was all to the good as it made for a darker night. At eight o'clock I again came out of the barn, this time with Les and two others who had agreed to make the attempt with us (one was a young American airman who had been shot down over Vienna). The guard questioned us but was satisfied with my explanation that the other three were coming to assist in the potato boiling, which was taking an unconscionably long time. Once over to the shed it was no difficult matter to gain the house and get up to the attic, where we lay until about eleven o'clock.

We descended the stairs slowly and, on emerging from the house, found that it was now so dark that we could not see the guard at the barn door. So providing we did not make too much noise we should be able to get away safely.

One of the Italians came out with us and gave us directions as to how to get out of the village, which was the most dangerous part since there were quite a few *Wehrmacht* soldiers about from our own column as well as some others whom we had noticed as we marched in. We were very grateful to our informer as he was taking a great risk in helping us, one that would probably have cost him his life if we had been caught with him.

We took our leave of our friend and hopped over the wall separating the farm buildings from the road, making a great clatter with our boots on the cobblestones. We stood still for a moment, and then started marching out of the village two abreast. We had only gone a few yards when we heard voices advancing towards us. It was useless stopping so we carried on and two figures passed us in the gloom. We could hear mess tins rattling, and guessed they were probably two of our guards on their way to supper. Thanks to the drizzle and the dark night they were only figures in the dark, so we must have been the same, and felt afterwards that it was our purposeful march in step that caused them to ignore us.

We met only one other person on our way out, a woman who passed quite close and must have recognised us for what we were. But although she would certainly have been a German to be out at night, she said nothing and took no notice. Possibly she was a little frightened by four enemy soldiers, but more probably she was not interested and just minding her own business.

Once outside the village we took to the fields. Our object was to get as near the front line as possible and, in the event of it proving impossible to get through, we would find some barn and hide up until the Americans came.

The cloud-darkened skies that had proved so friendly in our getaway were now a severe hindrance, since we could get no idea of direction from the stars. We had counted on being led by the sound of gunfire, which we had heard earlier in the evening, but it had now died down and after about half-an-hour's steady going across ploughed fields we stopped and held a whispered consultation. Apart from the drone of a night patrol plane high above us, all was silent as the grave — a fact that enjoined us to extreme caution, since it meant that the merest whisper could be heard some distance away.

The first decision we had to make was on the question of cover. Were we to go into the woods or keep to the open country? We were divided on this — Jack (the American airman) and Mitch favouring the woods, whereas Les and I wanted to stay in open country. It was our opinion that while the cover afforded by the woods was obvious and desirable, with the front line only a few miles away it was certain that they were patrolled, if only sporadically, by German troops. In the end we had our way and we continued in the open, this time keeping near to the road in the hope of eventually getting some idea of direction.

We continued in this manner until the first signs of dawn were manifest, skirting villages and farmhouses, always looking for an isolated barn in which we might hide during daylight hours. We tried the doors of several barns on the outskirts of villages, but all were securely locked, and dawn found us still in the open. We were not at all displeased to see the dawn since it gave us a definite direction, and all we wanted now was a nice comfortable barn.

We were at this time in an open part of the country with not even a small hayrick in sight and all we could do was to press on quickly towards the west, hoping that something would turn up before we were spotted. We were, of course, still in our battle-dress uniforms; but over these we had Army greatcoats — which were not unlike the brown overcoat worn by some Nazi organizations — so we stood a chance of getting away with it if anybody saw us at a distance. We were, of course, instantly recognisable at anything up to 50 yards.

Finally we saw a small village in the distance with a large wood behind it. We decided to make for this village and try to force a barn somewhere on the outskirts of the place. If we were unsuccessful we should have no alternative but to go into the woods, as to stay in the open in broad daylight was obviously impossible.

Suddenly there appeared in front of us, on the road about 100 yards away, a group of men with shovels over their shoulders. Their approach had been hidden from us by a dip in the ground, and with open fields on both sides of us there was nothing for us to do but carry on walking and hope for the best.

As they neared us we saw that they had armbands on which

proclaimed them as members of the *Volksturm* (Home Guard), probably going out to dig trenches. They drew level with us and we kept going. They looked curiously and I said 'Good Morning,' although I felt it was going to be anything but a good morning if they challenged us. They did not answer, but nor did they stop, and we were suffered to continue unmolested, although with many backward glances on both their side and ours.

We passed through a small village in the dip which had been previously out of sight, passing on our way three *Volksturm* village guards — none of whom attempted to stop us although they were obviously wondering who the devil we were. It was now broad daylight and every moment we stayed out of cover was dangerous.

We neared the village we had previously spotted and, seeing that everyone was already astir, decided it was too dangerous to attempt to go nearer. Here, however, good fortune attended us and we saw a barn by the side of a road running parallel to the one we were on, about 300 yards to our right. In full sight of the village, we crossed the fields and gained it. It seemed, and still seems to me, impossible that nobody from the village saw us, and why we were not arrested in the barn is a mystery to me. I can only suppose that the nearness of the Americans gave the villagers other things to think about than the possibility of escaped prisoners of war hiding near their homes.

The barn was not a big one, filled to a height of about ten feet each side of the doors with straw. We climbed up and, burrowing under the straw, were soon all asleep.

We woke at about midday to the sound of thousands of marching feet. Through a crack in the wall of the barn we could see column after column of *Luftwaffe* ground troops marching eastward, interspersed with Russian prisoners of war whose camps were in the line of advance and whom the Germans were trying to get away to a place of safety.

We debated our course of action. We all realised that we were much safer where we were, but it might be a week before the Americans actually took this particular stretch of road and we had no food. We half decided that two of us should try and get up to the village to see whether there was any chance of getting anything to eat, and I started putting on my boots, which I had taken off before settling down that morning.

Everyone knows the noise straw makes as it is rustled and Les suddenly enjoined me to be still. Three men were coming into the barn. We all kept quiet and heard them settle down just inside the doorway, apparently to have something to eat.

From the conversation it appeared they were SS men; their unit had been split up by the previous day's fighting and they were retreating on their own. The American tank spearhead they said, was only 11 kilometres away, but that news, though cheering, was no indication of how far away the main forces were. The front line must still be some distance from where we were, as the sound of gunfire sounded much fainter than we thought it ought to sound.

The men stayed more than half an hour, during which time my three companions lay still where they were in the straw. I too, was still, but in no such comfortable position; I had one boot half on and was in a half-sitting, half-kneeling position. By the time the three men went out of the barn I was stiff with cramp.

We got ready as quickly as possible, but by this time more troops were passing and we had to stay where we were until they had gone by. During this wait we heard rifle shots quite close to us in the wood, the fringe of which was only a couple of hundred yards from the barn. Since no American troops could be this close it was pretty plain that someone was being shot, and we realised that the barn was by no means as safe as we had thought. After another discussion therefore, we determined to move.

Since the woods and roads were swarming with troops of all kinds now, it was obviously impossible to attempt to remain unseen once we left the barn, so we decided to stay on the road and try to bluff it out.

Our story would be, if challenged, that we were prisoners of war from a camp near the front line. The guards had marched the camp away in one of the usual columns but as we were all lame, we had fallen behind and were now trying to catch them up. A bit thin possibly, but the story might pass in the immediate confusion. The trouble was that it was now impossible for us to go westward toward the front line, since such a move would not tally with our story. Apart from that, with the now known presence of SS men in the vicinity such a move would have been little short of suicidal. Our only hope was that we could move slowly enough for the Americans to catch us up, and with this in mind we once more took to the road.

We had only gone a little way when we fell in with some men wearing the uniform of the *Organisation Todt*, the German military pioneers. We told them our story but they evinced no interest and evidently didn't care whether we went with them or not. Certainly they were not in the mood to be bothered to hand us over to any military authority. We thought we would be better on our own so we let them get well in front of us and, as we came to the point of the road where it passed into a large wood, were once more on our own.

The OT men had just passed out of sight round a bend in the road when, round the same bend, came about 20 men on bicycles, all with the *Volksturm* brassard on their arms and rifles slung across their backs. They all looked at us intently as they drew near and the leader slowed up as he called out, 'Who are you and where do you come from?'

I pointed vaguely along the road and muttered something about the column having gone on, but while I was trying to frame a suitable reply a man in the centre of the group called out to the leader, 'That's not them. They're prisoners alright, but they can't be escaping — they're going eastward!' and with this the group cycled on. We had obviously had a narrow escape, and this incident proved the value of the plan of moving eastward instead of westward, which was the direction we really wanted.

There was one further minor incident during this part of our walk; an American army co-operation plane which had been circling over the area almost all morning, suddenly dived and machine-gunned the road in front of us. It was quite a good way in front and no bullets came near us, but the incident was a trifle discomforting and a reminder that on the road we stood in just as much danger from our own side as we did from the enemy.

After some time we emerged from the wood and the road led into a little village, the chief building of which was an old chateau which was now being used as a military hospital. We walked straight into the village and would not have been questioned had it not been for the presence of some Russian prisoners who were resting on the far side of it.

In the middle of the village, just outside the entrance to the hospital, the road turned a right-angle and suddenly brought into our view a group of about 30 Russian prisoners with their guards, resting on a bank at the side of the road just outside the village about 100 yards further on from us. We halted immediately, for if we were picked up now, we would probably be handed over to the guards of the Russians and made to continue the march with them.

Seeing our obvious hesitation, a German corporal who was standing nearby talking to a young sea cadet, called out and asked what we wanted. Les and I walked over to him and I told him that we were prisoners who had fallen behind our column but were all too lame to catch up with it. This, I hoped, would scotch any ideas of tagging us on to the Russian column.

At this, the young sea cadet whose name was Karl, said that he would be delighted to assist us and led us into the hospital grounds. We were a bit dubious about the outcome of this, but in any case we could not do anything about it so we followed him.

He took us into a little room beside the disused stables and asked us what he could do for us. We said we wanted a wash and something to eat and he supplied us with a bucket of water and went off to see what could be done to procure some food. While he was gone we had a wash and shave (we had soap, shaving kit and towels in our pockets) and discussed the situation.

Our position was a curious one. We were in a German military hospital, with German troops and civilians moving all around us. We were recognised as Englishmen and yet we were still not officially recognised. Until we were actually apprehended and handed over to either the military or the police we still stood a chance, albeit a much reduced one, of getting away again. Even this chance seemed to fade away when Karl came back and told us that our story was not believed and the corporal had reported our presence to the hospital authorities. But we clung to the hope that fortune, which had favoured us this far, would continue to do so. And so it worked out. From this time onward our good luck held with a consistency which was little short of amazing, and lucky coincidences piled one on top of the other in a manner that would not be believed in a novel.

Karl was our good Samaritan at that hospital. He had persuaded his father to cook us some potatoes and even found us some bean soup from somewhere, as well as lighting a fire for us in the little room. He was just 16 and had entered the navy academy for three years. Now, however, realising that the war was already lost, he had torn his eagle and swastika from his uniform and was hoping against hope that when the Americans took his villag, they would treat him as a civilian youth and not as a hard-bitten naval SS man, which his badges would have proclaimed him to be.

After we had eaten our fill of potatoes he took me for a walk around the hospital grounds. It was so peaceful standing by the little lake in the grounds that it seemed impossible that a war was going on only ten or twenty miles away, but I was forcibly reminded of it when Karl pointed to the sky. Coming out of a white cloud high above our heads was a large group of silver planes and these were followed by more, until there were several hundred in sight at one time. I had never before seen so many planes, and no Allied planes for five years, and was quite cheered to see that we actually had some.

We stayed in the hospital until about six o'clock, during which time several old men from the village came in to see us and tell us that they 'hadn't wanted the war really.' Then Karl, who had been out scouting for news for us, came in with a long face and we knew he had bad news.

'The hospital authorities have telephoned the Chief of Police in Badeckenstedt,' he told us, 'and a man in the village has been instructed to take you there now and hand you over to him.'

This certainly was not good news, as we had been hoping to

be allowed to remain at the hospital until the Americans took it, protected while we were inside by the Red Cross. But it was not to be helped and since we had eaten we felt much better than we had the night before.

A farmer arrived at the gates with a horse and cart, and after taking our leave of Karl, whose help we had really appreciated, we climbed in and were driven away.

The farmer seemed quite cheerful and we began to be suspicious of him. We wondered whether the column was still near enough for him to be able to take us back to it, which was the very last thing we wanted, and as we neared Badeckenstedt these suspicions became almost a certainty. While we had been on the march during the past three months, it had been usual for the German officer in charge of the column to go ahead and chalk the route up on walls or signposts wherever there was a divergence of roads. This was done by means of an arrow and the figures 4/714 — i.e. the fourth company of No. 714 battalion — and we could see these figures on every signpost we passed on the way to Badeckenstedt. As it happened, it was no more than a coincidence that the column had passed through the very town to which we were now being taken, but naturally we did not know this at the time and we debated the idea of knocking the driver on the head when we passed through the next set of woods. The woods came and went, and it was obvious none of us was going to hit this poor old chap on the head.

When we got to Badeckenstedt we drove right through the town and stopped outside the very last house. This was the private house of the local Chief of Police, who, it appeared, was known personally to the driver of the cart (who was, incidentally, still quite cheerful with us and rather amused by our wanderings on our own). He went up the stairs and knocked at the door. After a brief talk with the woman who opened to him he returned to the cart looking a little crestfallen. The Chief of Police was away it appeared, and so were all the policemen, and he (the farmer) had no time to go scouring the town for any of them as he had his farm to consider. And anyway his evening meal would be getting cold.

It was, we told him, unthinkable that he should eat a cold supper on our account and we were ready to assist him. If he would leave us there, he could go back to his farm and his supper and we would wait where we were until the Chief of Police came home, when we would report to him. Was that not an excellent idea? He thought it was, although he was at first a little dubious. Finally the supper won and after tapping him for a cigarette apiece, we allowed him to depart homewards, leaving us standing by the roadside to wait for the police to arrive and lock us up.

As soon as he was out of sight we started off along the road leading away from the town. About 200 yards further on we came to a fork in the road — one road, obviously the main one, leading straight on and the other branching off to the left. We looked on the signpost and saw the 4/714 sign with an arrow pointing along the main road, so we turned off to the left.

A short way along this road, which sloped gently upwards away from the main road, we met a little civilian going down towards the town. He stopped, stared at us, and then asked if we were Poles, Czechs or any other brand of Allied soldier. We said we were Englishmen and an American, and he flung his arms round the nearest man (it happened to be me) and kissed me on both cheeks. From which it will be gathered he was a Frenchman.

His name was Louis and he had come out of a cinema in Paris one evening in 1941 and had been led straight to a waiting lorry, which bore him and several other unfortunates straight to the railway station, whence he entrained at once for Germany. Since that day he had not seen France again, and the knowledge that final liberation was now not far off made him more than ever glad to see us.

He expressed himself ready to help us if he could and asked us how we had got there. We told him the story of the lame men who could not keep up with the column, for we had not forgotten that there were still two kinds of Frenchmen.

He took us up into the village of Gross Elbe, about a mile off the main road, and in the middle of the village we came upon the little barbed-wire enclosure that betrays the presence of a Prisoner of War Working Camp. This particular one housed 36 Serbs, who had been here since their capture in Yugoslavia in 1941, and there was only one guard in charge of them. If the Americans came the Serbs would not be taken away, as the Germans only thought it worthwhile getting the Englishmen, Russians and Americans away when a prison camp was in danger of being overrun by the enemy. All this Louis told us, and as we came up to the little camp the guard came out of the house to see who we were and what we wanted.

We told him our usual story, and said we wanted to rest here in his prison camp for the night before continuing in the morning to try to catch our column. He shook his head. He didn't want us. Here we were, escaping enemy soldiers, and he didn't want to let us into his prison camp! We weren't on the strength.

Suddenly this camp seemed a desirable place to be, and I started arguing with him for admission. The matter was settled by two of the Serbs, coming out of the door inside the wire compound and seeing us.

They ran up to us and asked who we were. When we told them they called out to their comrades, who came running up;

after two words of explanation, these all combined in pushing us into the compound, while one of their number took the guard aside, presumably to assure him that everything would be all right.

It is difficult to describe the scene that took place inside the building. Had we been members of a liberating army we could not have been made more welcome. The good Serbs could not do enough for us. They clapped us on the back, miraculously produced American cigarettes for us to smoke, offered us all in one breath new boots, clothes, food; each one wanted the honour of sleeping on the floor so that we could have his bed. They shouted, they cheered, they sang; one of them produced an accordion and commenced to play. They were the happiest group of men I had seen in years. And all this because we were English and American.

Escape 1945 — the Serb camp

That evening they prepared us a meal made out of a concoction of their rations and a couple of Red Cross tins of fish. It tasted delicious, and they were highly delighted when we told them so. Actually, this meal in itself represented a great sacrifice on their part; they did not receive a Red Cross parcel a week as we had done, but like all other Allied prisoners (excepting the Russians) they got one parcel per month from either the British or the American Red Cross Society, and since they, like ourselves, had had no parcels for over three months, this meal was, as I say, a great sacrifice. They would not hear of a refusal, however, and in truth we were in no position to refuse food from wherever it came as, having marched nearly 800 miles on a starvation diet, we were in a state of continuous hunger. That night, however, we ate our fill and when we had finished one of the Serbs produced a bottle of wine from somewhere with which we all drank each other's health.

The camp barber gave us a haircut, the camp cobbler gave my three companions a mended pair of boots (I didn't think it worthwhile taking new boots from them myself as we would almost certainly be liberated in a few days), and from all sides they pressed cigarettes they had saved from their last parcel, while they themselves smoked some home-grown leaf. It was impossible to refuse them since a refusal obviously hurt their feelings and an acceptance delighted them, and we smoked until we were dry.

The building in which they were billeted was part of the village *Gasthouse*, and had apparently originally been a concert hall in more peaceful times. The *Gasthouse* itself belonged to one Friedrich Brand, who also owned a small farm nearby, and this Brand was responsible for the prisoners in the absence of the guard. Each of the prisoners worked for a different farmer in the village, Brand himself employing only one of them. He and the guard came in to see us during the course of the evening, mainly to assure himself that we intended moving on in the morning. Actually we had no intention at all of doing so if we could avoid it, but to make sure of at least one night there we promised we would. The morrow would have to look after itself.

When they had gone and the billet was locked up, the Serbs moved a cupboard in the corner and produced from behind it a number of maps of Germany, and we all gathered round the table to see if we could work out the nearness of the Americans. We were confident that they would be here the following morning, since reports had been coming in all day from villagers who had been in the town that the American tanks had been seen only six kilometres away. We learned later that the tanks which had been seen were from a column that was making its way along the other side of the Harz mountains, but this we did not know of course, and we counted on seeing them much earlier than they could really be expected.

During the course of the evening we got to know several of the Serbs, and one of them in particular stands out in memory. This was Nickolitch, who was the interpreter, man-of-confidence, and sergeant-major of the camp all in one. He thoroughly merited the confidence his comrades had in him, as he was easily the best-educated in the camp — a good leader, a thoroughly likeable man, and very popular with everybody.

I never saw in any English camp such authority combined with popularity as he commanded; he had only to give an order and it was obeyed instantly and gladly, though it must be borne in mind that we saw the camp under favourable conditions, since with liberation in sight, everyone was happy and thought every-one else a thoroughly good fellow.

Another notable man was Milos, who appeared to be Nickolitch's particular friend, and these two did their best to outdo everybody else in showing hospitality to their four visitors.

Escape 1945 — helpers Nikolitch and Milos

That night we each slept in one of their bunks. We felt most uncomfortable about this, since it meant that eight of them had to sleep squeezed together two to a bunk to make four bunks empty for us. But they would not have it otherwise and finally, tiring of arguing with them, we took to the beds and were soon asleep.

The following day was Saturday, and early in the morning the guard came in and asked if we were ready to go. We told him that we were not and he said we must be ready by nine o'clock. He was going to his Company HQ in the town and when he came back we would have to go.

We discussed this with our Serbian friends. They were sympathetic but could offer no advice. They took their leave of us and went out to work, leaving us alone in the billet to await the return of the guard at nine o'clock.

It may appear strange that we should be so anxious to remain in a prison camp when we had been at such pains to escape from one, but actually we were better off there than we would have been on the road. Once outside this camp, we were liable at any time to be arrested by police or recaptured by the military, or even by the SS, in which latter case we would almost certainly have been shot. Here, however, we could live in comparative comfort and safety, and when the Americans came we would be liberated. We had already ascertained from the Serbs that Louis's information the day before had been correct and the camp would not be shifted under any circumstances. We were therefore determined that unless the guard threatened to shoot us if we didn't leave we were going to stay where we were. We need not have worried. Lady Luck was still looking after us...

At nine the guard returned and asked us if we were ready to go. We said no, and what was he going to do about it? But he had no time to argue with us. He had, he told us, been to his Company HQ — but the Company wasn't there anymore!

It was obvious what had happened. The Company was beating a hasty retreat, and we told him so. He seemed a little doubtful as to what to do, so I told him the best thing for him was to pack up his kit and follow the Company. If he moved fast enough, he might even catch them up. He too thought that was the best course, and within ten minutes he was shaking hands with us and saying goodbye, with full kit on his back and his rifle over his shoulder. He called in Herr Brand and handed over the camp to him, telling him he could do what he liked with us. Then he was gone and we were left to deal with Friedrich.

Although we later got on quite well with him, Friedrich was at first difficult to handle. He, like all other Germans, was very much afraid of Authority, and in this instance he feared that if Authority, in the shape of the police or the army, found out that we were hiding on his farm with his knowledge he would get into trouble. Nor could we convince him that Authority had too many other worries at the moment to bother with a few escaped prisoners of war. He was adamant. We must go.

We refused. I pointed out that as enemy prisoners of war we were not allowed on the road without a guard, and since there was definite danger at the moment in being out by ourselves, we could not go unless he provided a guard to take us. He had, as we well knew, no guard and no means of getting one, so seeing himself up against a brick wall he went to fetch the *Burgermeister*.

We awaited the *Burgermeister* with some trepidation, for such people are inclined to be authoritative, and it was quite probable that he would hand us over to the police. When he arrived with Friedrich, however, he proved to be a benevolent old farmer and not at all displeased to see us.

'What do you want here?' he asked.

Since it was fairly obvious what we wanted I told him. We wanted to stay where we were until the Americans came near enough for us to get to them, or better still, until they took the village itself. He turned to Herr Brand.

'You see Friedrich,' he said, clapping the *Gasthouse* keeper on the shoulder, 'all they want is to get to the Americans, who are their friends. If you had been a prisoner as long as they have, you'd want to see your friends as well. Of course they shall stay.

You arrange for your wife to give them food and I'll send over a few tins of meat to help you out.'

So that was that. We thanked the *Burgermeister* suitably and off he went. He was as good as his word, and a few minutes later he sent over two four-pound tins of corned meat for us. Friedrich too, was now all smiles. The matter had been taken out of his hands by someone who could be held responsible, and he himself was quite prepared to be as friendly as we wished. His wife — a fat, cheerful old German *Hausfrau* — cooked us some soup, and we settled down perfectly content to await the coming of the Yanks.

That afternoon the *Burgermeister* took steps to ensure the safety of his village. The sole defence of the locality was in the hands of the *Volksturm*, local farmers with armbands for a uniform and old rifles or shotguns for weapons. The *Burgermeister*, realising the futility of resistance, collected in all the weapons to make sure no fanatic started a fight, and hung out a large white flag from the tower of the village church. When Nickolitch and his comrades came in at midday they were as excited as schoolchildren, and once more we had to indulge in an orgy of smoking to please them.

Friedrich came in several times during the evening. He was, it appeared, worried in case we were still there the next week. He could not, he said, afford to feed us unless we worked, and although he was willing to be obliging and keep us until the German troops in the area decided whether they were going to advance or retreat, he thought it was only right that we should work while we were with him. We were confident that we would no longer be there by Monday morning, so we agreed to work for him during the week with the other Serbian prisoners. It had always been a joke amongst we prisoners how much the German mind runs on work, but although I was accustomed to this way of thinking I was nevertheless amazed during the following two days to see how indifferent the Germans were during working hours to the war going on around them.

The following morning was Sunday, and since the Serbs did not work on Sundays we spent the morning sitting out in the tiny compound enjoying the early spring sunshine and singing to the accompaniment of Milos on his accordian. Mitch was an excellent accordionist, and the Serbs were highly delighted when he took the accordian from Milos and played some English tunes.

Les and I went for a walk with Nickolitch in the village before lunch, with half a dozen other Serbs trailing behind us. We met several of the villagers, some of whom had already heard that there were Englishmen in the village and some who had not. None of them expressed any surprise at our presence, and we had several invitations to *Mittagessen*. These we declined, deeming it wiser to stay under the protective roof of Herr Brand. Although the Serbs were still as excited as ever, we were becoming a little apprehensive. For two days now the Americans had been continually reported as being 'only six kilos away,' and still they had not arrived. Certainly it seemed as though nothing could go wrong now, and in fact we had counted on a delay of a day or two. All four of us had made unsuccessful attempts to escape on previous occasions, and we were afraid to count our chickens before they were hatched in case some unforeseen circumstance cropped up and robbed us of our freedom, which appeared to be in sight. One disturbing fact was that the white flag had been taken down from the village church due, we learned, to the arrival of an SS Major who had threatened to shoot the *Burgermeister* unless he removed it.

That afternoon we were treated to the sound of war on three

sides of us, the nearest 'show' being not more than two miles away.

The village was on the slope of a hill with a large wood, semircular in shape, forming the horizon on three sides — the fringe of the wood being between a mile and about four miles away. During the afternoon an artillery duel began in the wood to the east of us, about eight or ten miles away we judged. Heavy rifle fire and machine-gun fire was going on about four miles away in the wood immediately to the north, while to the north-west, almost on top of the village it seemed, three USA light fighter-bombers were bombing the wood, which was on fire at this point. It was encouraging to see that the front was not far away, although in modern mobile warfare a single point of action is not necessarily indicative of a front. We now began to wonder whether German troops would occupy the village when they started retreating, in which case it would almost certainly be bombed out of existence. That, however, remained to be seen and we did not worry much about it.

The following morning there was still no sign of the Americans, nor of any war for that matter, and since one Monday morning was no different to any other to Herr Brandt we prepared to go out to work. Jack, the airman, was to work for the saddler in the village, while Mitch, Les and I were to remain with Freidrich. We learned from Nickolitch that the *Burgermeister* of Badeckenstedt, realising that there was no longer any hope of the town being saved from occupation by the enemy, had ordered the warehouses and factories to be thrown open to the public, as well as issuing out the coal briquettes which were loaded in several wagons standing in the railway sidings. Freidrich was taking his two carts down to the town to load them up with briquettes before it was too late, and accordingly, we harnessed them up.

To our surprise, the carts were drawn by cows. I had never seen this before but I understood it was common practice in many parts of Germany.

We were not too keen on this trip to Badeckenstedt. We hoped to pass for Serbs, but if we were recognised as Englishmen by anyone in authority, it was too much to hope that we would be treated as well as we had been by the *Burgermeister* of Gross Elbe. We borrowed Serbian forage caps from our friends, but it was a pretty meagre 'disguise.' We could only hope that everyone would be too busy to worry about us. And so it was.

There was quite a lot of activity among the civilians in the town, but we did not see many soldiers. Of those we saw, only the SS seemed to be moving up to the front. The *Wehrmacht* men were visible in ones and twos, usually with all their kit on their backs, but it was difficult to know whether this meant that they were marching up to the front with their unit, retreating with a unit, or just sliding off on their own. (Despite the confusion in the fighting by this time, early April 1945, the latter was not very likely. Deserters got very short shrift from the Field Police.)

The three of us were taken to the railway sidings, where a queue of people were waiting their turn to receive a ration of coal brickettes from one of the railway wagons; it was all being done in a very orderly manner. It was really looting, but orderly looting.

I found myself among some civilians putting our shoulders to a railway wagon to push it a bit further along the line, and my neighbour on this little pushing stint told me there was a rumour there were some English escapers in the town. He thought that was one of them pointing to Les. This was quite amusing, as Les had pulled his Serbian cap right down over his head in the belief that this constituted a complete disguise. The man may have been trying to draw me, as, although I also had one of these caps, the rest was British battledress, but nothing further happened.

Friedrich Brandt was there, and called me over to say the briquettes were loaded, and he would come back with the wagon with Mitch and Les. I was to go ahead on my own.

And so, after years behind barbed wire, I walked right through the town of Badeckenstedt in the middle of a war, in British uniform, on busy pavements with soldiers and civilians about their business, and although I got a few curious glances, not a soul stopped me. I walked past the house of the Chief of Police where we were supposed to have waited to be arrested, out of the town, up to the lane to Gross Elbe, into the Serbs' prison camp, which now had the gate permanently open, and sat down to await the return of Herr Brandt.

In due course the other three turned up, then the Serbs, back from their day's work, and in the evening, the *Burgermeister*. He had come on a most friendly visit, to show us a cellar which was to be used as an air raid shelter should the occasion arise. There had been no air raids on Gross Elbe so far (not surprising, this tiny village was hardly a primary target), but it was there, just in case. Our *Burgermeister* friend showed us with some pride the stout timbers that had been used to give additional support to the cellar roof; if there was an air raid we were to come down there with him where we would be safe.

Oddly enough, we all used that shelter that night — the first and last time in the war it ever served its purpose. There was no air raid, but rather an artillery duel between German and American guns that night, with Gross Elbe in between. There was really no danger, except for the outside possibility of a short drop, as the shells were passing well overhead, but Brandt came into the camp — not perhaps in panic, but certainly very agitated — and ushered us all down to the *Burgermeister's* cellar. It was quite large and we could all sit down. We stayed there for an hour or so, then Mitch, Les, Jack and I all went up again into the deserted camp and laid down on the beds. Later some of the Serbs came up as well, but most of them stayed in the cellar well into the early hours. I think Brandt stayed there all night, long after the firing ceased.

The following morning we went out of the gates to find the *Burgermeister*. Brandt and some other civilians already out there. There was a very heavy mist, with visibility perhaps only about 50 yards. There was also a continuous sound, which even I could hear, although not as clearly as the others. Down on the main road was the rumble of heavy and continuing traffic, and our *Burgermeister* friend Brandt and the others were debating the question of what should be done, if anything, to find out what it was. The fact was, of course, that Brandt and the rest wanted it to be the arrival of the Americans just as much as we did, but what if it was the German army, either retreating or even moving up for some counter-attack? Having put his white sheets out in the village, and then having had to take them down again, the mayor wanted no risk of getting involved with rival armies. All he wanted to do was to put out the white flags again, but he dared not do so until he was sure of what was down there on the road, barely a mile away and normally visible from the village but hidden now by the strong morning mist.

We certainly wanted to know what it was, and the upshot of the deliberation was the dispatch of the four escapers to find out. We started from the edge of the village where the road started its long dip down to the main road, and it seemed half the village had turned out to see us off, as if we were intrepid explorers about to venture into the unknown.

The revelation was as dramatic as it ought to have been. We walked down the road together, still in mist with nothing to be seen ahead. Then suddenly, as we neared the main road with the noise of traffic now very loud, the mist lifted.

Ahead on the main road, barely 200 yards away, was an unbroken stream of heavy lorries almost nose to tail, a white star on the side of each.

It was the American Army.

Epilogue

We hitch-hiked for three days through the American lines into the British sector and eventually arrived at Brussels, where we were put up for the night in a hotel earmarked for returning prisoners of war once the mass was liberated. At this time it had only a dozen guests, all escapers like ourselves. We were told that we would be flown home the next day, and in the meantime could enjoy a night out. We were given £5 in Belgian money (later deducted from pay), and with this Les and I went out on the town.

It can be imagined how much this first free night had been discussed in the prison camps. Wine, women and song, there would be no holding us. Here was the ideal situation to put this into effect; Brussels was a leave town for British troops, and in the bars and the dance-halls the girls were everywhere.

We wandered around disconsolately for a couple of hours, had a beer or two, and with perfect mutual understanding, went back to the hotel. This was simply not the object of the exercise. The object was to get back to England, and we were not there yet. When we got back to the hotel I went to bed, but Les took no chances of missing the plane and stayed up all night.

The following morning we were flown home, spent one day being deloused, equipped with new uniforms and all the paraphernalia of unfamiliar ration books, coupons, dockets and the rest, and then went on leave. I left Les at King's Cross Station — he to go home to Hull, and I to go home in North London.

Although a Yorkshireman, Les was engaged to a London girl, and a few months later I had the privilege of being his best man when he came down to London to marry her and take her back to Hull, where they both had a long and happy marriage. Sadly, Les died of cancer in 1980.

That good soldier and medic, Spud Taylor, survived the war by 20 years, and was killed in a motor accident.

Phin Phillips remained a bachelor and was a frequent visitor to our home for many years. Unfortunately he gradually became generally downcast and pessimistic; he lived into his eighties, and died alone.

Denis Hoy had a happier story; he married Joan and is still enjoying life, garden and an interest in local societies in Enfield in Middlesex.

And I? I went home on six weeks' leave to a wife of five years, with whom I had spent five days of married life five years ago. We had of course both changed, and both of us had long felt that if I survived this war the marriage should be ended so that we could both make a fresh start. We therefore agreed that we would spend my leave together in a last holiday, and then separate and arrange a divorce. We had our holiday, but were back in London for VE day in Piccadilly Circus. Then we parted — Doris to go to her aunt and I back to the army, where I would be utterly useless and only awaiting demobilisation.

The next week I returned. I had changed my mind, and went to ask Doris to come back. I am not sure what thought predominated in this. Perhaps I did not want the bother of a divorce, a harder process in those days than now; perhaps it was just male ego, taking umbrage that she wanted to end the marriage as much as I did. Perhaps I loved her after all.

A little reluctantly, she agreed to give it a trial. So Doris came back and for the next 37 years, until her death in 1982, I enjoyed the companionship, the support and the love of the most wonderful wife a man could have. If in doubt, ask any of our four daughters.

Fours years after Doris died I met and married Barbara, acquired two more daughters and have since enjoyed ten years of a greater happiness than most men can expect or deserve.

Marriage to Barbara, June 1986

With Denis Hoy at the Rifle Memorial at Calais.
50th anniversary of Calais Battle, May, 1990.

About the Author

Edward 'Ted' Lyme was born in Hackney in 1918, and grew up in London's East End, the son of a bus conductor. When the Second World War began in 1938/39, Ted joined the King's Royal Rifle Corps at Winchester, but was soon transferred to the Queen Victoria's Rifles. During the Defence of Calais in 1940 – a diversionary Allied attack to draw the German forces away from Dunkirk in order to enable the evacuation – Ted was captured after just two days of active service, and spent the next five years as a prisoner of war. Over the years he escaped his captors three times, was successful on his third attempt, and eventually reached England just six weeks before the end of the war in 1945. He subsequently settled in Chalfont St. Peter to the Northwest of London, became a successful family man and entrepreneur (founding his own thriving manufacturing business), and was a Parish and County Councillor for thirty years. He died, age 91, on November 14th, 2009 – a dearly loved father, stepfather, grandfather and great grandfather.

Printed in Great Britain
by Amazon